Power Surge

A Conduit for Enlightened Leadership

Margaret Seidler

HRD Press, Inc. ▪ Amherst ▪ Massachusetts

Published by: HRD Press, Inc.
22 Amherst Road
Amherst, Massachusetts 01002
1-800-822-2801 (U.S. and Canada)
1-413-253-3488
1-413-253-3490 (fax)
http://www.hrdpress.com

ISBN: 978-1-59996-162-0

Polarity Map and the Infinity Loop and Two Poles © 1992, 2008
Polarity Management Associates, LLC

Polarity Management Associates acknowledges the following contributors to the Polarity Map:
    Credit for Infinity Loop element: Sallie Snyder
    Credit for Greater Purpose element: John Scherer, The Scherer Leadership Center
    Credit for Synergy Arrows element: De Wit and Meyer BV

Editorial services by Suzanne Bay
Production services by Anctil Virtual Office
Cover design by Eileen Klockars

This book is dedicated to the memory of two sisters:

June Dandridge Thorne
and
Mamie Dandridge Thomas

My mother June and my aunt Mamie were as different as night and day, poles apart in how they lived their lives and how they interacted with others. Despite those differences, they were close friends and sisters all their lives, and taught me much of what I needed to know in order to succeed in my own life. From June, I learned how to be strong and go after what I wanted. From Aunt Mamie, I learned how to care for and help others. For many years, those two values seemed to be an unlikely combination. Today, it makes a lot of sense.

Contents

Acknowledgments

This book would not be possible without the help and support of Herb Frazier, who spent hours with me crafting the story.

I wish to thank Dr. Barry Johnson for all he has taught me and shared so generously. The Polarity Map is based on the work of Polarity Management Associates.

The inspiration for this book came from Yarrow Durbin of the Washington Courage and Renewal Center and her method of looking at motivational values.

Motivational value definitions and certain concepts for their use have been adapted for this publication from The Mandalan Quest Values Survey, and related processes, developed by Roger Bruce Marshall of Philemon-Joy & Associates, and used with his permission.

The utility business is highly technical. I received support from Jim Swittenberg of South Carolina Electric and Gas Company, and William Westbrook of the Fayetteville Public Works Commission.

I am also grateful for numerous friends, colleagues, and clients who read drafts and gave me constructive feedback.

Thank you all.

Foreword

Power Surge brings ancient wisdom to a modern world. The focus on interdependent pairs (polarities) is as old as Judaism (4,000 years), which recognizes an interdependency between a god of mercy who loves us *and* a god of justice who holds us accountable for our actions. One of the most universally recognized interdependent pairs comes from Taoism, a belief system as old as 2,500 years, which recognizes the interdependency between yin and yang. In other words, the notion of interdependent pairs or polarities is not new. It is ancient. It is also not new in the lives of each of you reading this book. Children as early as two are taught to share their toys with the neighbor children and their brothers and sisters. Sharing is a means to manage the polarity of taking care of myself *and* taking care of others. So this book is about a subject not new to books or new to your life experience.

In 1975, I began working with a model and set of principles about these interdependent pairs which have become known as Polarity Management. Margaret Seidler has combined the polarity map and principles with motivational values in pairs to make a very user-friendly book for any person to tap this phenomena.

In the last fifty years, there has been a growing interest in the power of polarities as it relates to leadership and business success. Whether we use the term *paradox* or *dilemma* or *polarity,* the research is clear: Those leaders and organizations who are able to manage polarities well outperform those who don't.

Effective leaders manage the power of the *and.* Through a combination of experience, intuition, and hard-earned wisdom, these leaders develop the ability to look within complex issues, identify interdependent pairs in tension (polarities), and capitalize on that tension. We all have a degree of ability to manage polarities because they are such a central part of our daily lives. Yet most leaders lack an explicit model and set of principles to both enhance their skills with these issues and to collaborate with others to intentionally manage them better. The use of the Polarity Map is a great container for organizing and making explicit the wisdom that comes from experience.

In *Power Surge,* Margaret Seidler takes the basic principles of Polarity Management and translates them to raise self-awareness for both personal and work relationships. Polarity Management principles provide a broader view and give clarity to what makes us strong and potentially stronger. The principles apply if you're a leader of a company, an employee, a parent, or a partner to a significant other.

—BARRY JOHNSON
Founder, Polarity Management Associates

Introduction

Each of us holds a set of beliefs or motivational values. These are defining beliefs, principles, and standards that we hold dear. Motivational Values drive what we think, say, and do, and they ultimately shape how we interact with others in our lives. Some Motivational Values are adopted during our early years at home with our families; others we incorporate through experience. Our Motivational Values make us unique and provide us with the opportunity for great strength. This is where the paradox exists: Each Motivational Value that makes us strong also has the potential to make us weak. This is possible because most of us see a Motivational Value as singular and independent.

I learned through Polarity Management that each of my Motivational Values can guide my actions more effectively when viewed as part of an *interdependent* pair—two very different values that are connected and that need each other over time to achieve something greater. It's a case where the whole is greater than the sum of the parts in that each value in the pair brings a very different set of strengths. By identifying and tapping the strengths of both values in the pair, I gain higher performance and minimize the risk of my strengths becoming my weaknesses.

So how do we become aware of and face this complex challenge? How do we get the best from our strengths, acknowledge our weaknesses, and live life more productively?

We can do it by identifying and managing our Motivational Values using the interdependent-pairs perspective. The approach can be difficult because it requires us to recognize and accept a related interdependent value. As I reflect upon my own experience, I now believe that much of my difficulty came with the mere suggestion that there was another way—not just the one way I believed was "right." So a critical step in my development was to accept that, in the past, I had only part of the "right" answer.

In the book, I present four fictional characters facing a workplace crisis. After taking a glimpse into the circumstances they find themselves in, you will have an opportunity to coach those characters and to develop your skills in applying Polarity Management methodology. Finally, I'll share examples about my own use and explain how I use the technique, and give you a step-by-step guide for your own discovery.

A note or two about the book

Polarity Management and specific terms used to explain this approach will be highlighted for the purpose of this book.

No character or organization described in this book represents any specific person or organization.

Part I

Power Loss

Chapter One

Storm Watch

Tuesday

On her thirty-ninth birthday, just two years ago almost to the day, Morgan Hendrix entered the world of electric power. She was selected from a long list of candidates as the right "fit" for a traditional utility trying to modernize itself. A mentoring plan called for her to learn the entire operation within three to five years.

The plan gave her time to learn the complex business, but it also gave others time to get used to the idea of a female top executive. Morgan was excited about this opportunity and honored to be the person to break the so-called "glass ceiling."

At least, until six weeks ago. That's when her boss and mentor, Douglas Brown, suffered a sudden and fatal heart attack. She found herself the *de facto* head of this vast operation in the middle of hurricane season. In fact, a hurricane was already brewing in the tropics, expected to cross the Caribbean and potentially make a direct hit right here later in the week, in one of the most historic, picturesque, southeastern coastal communities in the United States.

To make matters worse, Morgan inherited some strong-willed department heads who clearly didn't understand the meaning of teamwork. She hadn't bargained for all this when she had agreed to be an apprentice at the region's largest electric utility.

With the death of Doug Brown and the approaching storm, she needed to move forward quickly. Given the amount of stress and grief the group would face, it would be a mammoth task to prepare for a major power outage and restoration should a hurricane make landfall.

She'd have to accomplish the planning and coordination with only three senior staff members. That's what worried her most: On the surface, they seemed like nice, well-intentioned and decent people, but she'd seen another side of them—a side where bickering and turf protection was the rule, not the exception. She was concerned about their inability to see their own weaknesses. They spent most of their time and energy shifting blame.

Morgan couldn't remember ever seeing a group perform so poorly together. She wondered why Doug Brown hadn't dealt with their conflicts. He had been a strong man in many other ways, but not when it came to resolving problems between people.

Despite the difficulties within the group, Morgan maintained her commitment to doing her job well. She felt an obligation and responsibility to the community. Citizens depended on the company to keep the lights on and certainly to get them back on quickly if there was an emergency outage.

Morgan worked hard for her achievements, and had the credentials to prove it. In trying to soften her entrance into this new world, she'd done her best to strike a note of humility. She decorated her office with simple art, rather than covering the walls with college degrees and certificates of accomplishment. She tried not to intimidate people or come across as arrogant. Friends had warned her that there would be gossip surrounding her selection as "heir apparent," but she took the job anyway because she knew it would lead to other career opportunities across the country.

As Morgan listened to the newscast update, she realized that it had been several decades since a major hurricane had made a direct hit on this part of the coast. Maybe the news reports were exaggerated about the size and force of the impending storm. Maybe people had become complacent. Anyway, it sounded like *this* storm was heading their way.

Her secretary had placed one of Doug Brown's files on her desk labeled "The Storm Plan." She decided to review it, quickly realizing that it was a blueprint to resolve damage and make repairs. As she read the report, she noticed a lack of detail and direction. Self-doubt began to creep into her thoughts. Mr. Brown's plan seemed out of date; it was designed only for a moderate storm, and it didn't account for the area's phenomenal growth over the past ten years.

Morgan hurriedly decided to direct the senior staff to redraw the storm plan. This represented her first major endeavor as their leader. She felt responsible for the greatly expanded and more complex electrical system, and needed to be assured that lives would not be lost in the aftermath of a storm due to downed power lines. She wanted to have a plan in place to get all the equipment and materials on-site.

This put in motion a series of rapid-fire questions: *How many transformers could blow in a storm? How many poles could be snapped in two like matchsticks? What about the large high-tension transmission lines in the rights-of-way? Could wind or trees cause damage to them? How would crews know where to report and where to make repairs?*

Power restoration would be complex, and would require complete cooperation across the workforce.

Morgan didn't want to be an alarmist, but she couldn't ignore the news reports. Unsure but resolved to lead, she asked her secretary to schedule a meeting with Kitty, Jerry, and William to plan for what might turn out to be the storm of the century.

She silently assessed the qualities of each of the senior staff members.

The Senior Staff

Kitty Lanier

Last year, Morgan helped Doug Brown hire Kitty Lanier as the HR director. Kitty came from a much larger company with far more staff and vast resources. Her master's degree was in Human Resource Development, but her work experience had consisted mostly of designing job interviewing and performance evaluation systems. She was thrilled to have been selected to manage an entire department, because it seemed like a great opportunity to make a difference. Friendly and instantly popular, Kitty was considered a true advocate for working men and women. Her popularity lay in her ability to connect with people and form relationships. Until her arrival, the electric utility had emphasized mostly logic and numbers. Tact and diplomacy came easy to Kitty because she didn't like to hurt people's feelings. She represented the new "soft" side, another key piece of the modernization strategy.

Jerry Manigault

Jerry Manigault, director of facilities and central stores (inventory), brought a wealth of experience as a thirty-five-year veteran at the utility. Tough and resilient, he had climbed through the ranks after starting out in the field as a lineman. He'd gone back to college at night and earned his degree while supporting a wife and four kids. Unlike Kitty, Jerry believed in the importance of being up front and candid with everyone. Rank made no difference to him—people always knew where he stood on every issue. However, his blunt remarks sometimes caused friction with others. Relationships came in last place when there was work to be done. Jerry subscribed to the motto *A fair day's wages for a fair day's work*. He believed people come to work to do the job, and he took that responsibility very seriously.

William Pringle

William Pringle was the utility's director of electric operations. He and Morgan shared a drive for results. Morgan secretly wanted to be more like him. A number of years ago, the utility worked with the local university to create a cooperative engineering program—a succession planning strategy critical to an industry facing waves of retirements in the coming decade. The program enabled young "high potentials" to rotate through different areas of the utility part-time while still in school. William started out in this program, and after graduation went full-time. Because of his drive and visibility across the utility, William rose quickly through the ranks. As the youngest person on the senior staff, he lacked the years of work experience of Kitty and Jerry, but he made up for it in confidence.

Morgan hoped she had everything under control. She couldn't stop the storm, but she could get ready for it—a daunting task. This would be her first major crisis.

She re-read the storm plan, shocked at its brevity:

Storm Assignments: Areas of Responsibility

Executive Manager (*Morgan Hendrix*)
- Coordination of all storm preparation and electrical restoration efforts
- Liaison with local elected officials and other government agencies
- Release of information to the media and the public

Director of Human Resources (*Kitty Lanier*)
- Mutual aid agreements with other utilities for additional personnel
- Provision of food and lodging for out-of-town workers, such as linemen and rights-of-way tree trimming crews

---

(continued)

In her previous jobs, Morgan had relied heavily on others for success. She'd always felt it was important to avoid rocking the boat, especially because she hated being perceived as the typically pushy stereotype of a female executive. Now, she'd have to rely on Kitty, Jerry, and William. *How can I exert professional will without looking arrogant?* She shuddered as she considered the consequences of failure.

Chapter Two

Storm Warning

Wednesday

Senior Staff Meeting

William was angry with Jerry. On their way into the meeting, they exchanged sharp words about transformers and poles on back-order.

William said, "Jerry, I just got a call from Joe. Where's that load of poles and transformers you promised for the crew quarters on Magnolia Road? What's going on over there in your department? What are you people doing? Haven't you gotten the paperwork completed for us?"

"What do you mean 'you people'?" Jerry snapped. "Don't put me in that category. I've worked hard for what I've gotten."

"This isn't about putting you down; this is about not doing your job," William said. "Those poles and transformers should have been here long ago. I hope you haven't dropped the ball on this. If you can't get it together, I'm going to Morgan."

"I don't think it's necessary for you to go to Morgan. We're big boys!" Jerry said sarcastically.

"Listen, I'm the one who's focused on the big picture here. You're stuck in the details. And I know how you people work."

"There you go with that 'you people' again."

Bickering was commonplace. Historically, the two departments, central stores and operations, had never cooperated very well. The recent build-up of conflict was now turning personal. William had inherited a strained relationship with Jerry from the last director of operations, but it had heightened and intensified. Many employees from the operations crews were offended by Jerry's unwillingness to update an old and cumbersome materials accounting system. In response, crews no longer followed Jerry's laborious recording procedures required for material check-out during night work or storm trouble. Even when crews did record the materials, they just guessed and often underestimated. The crews' ongoing behavior, which angered Jerry, caused him to misjudge when ordering. Thus, a sizeable gap existed between the materials he thought were on hand vs. actual in-stock inventory. Worse, he couldn't identify the missing items until it was too late, usually through a material request from operations. The unfulfilled utility-pole order for Magnolia Road proved that point again.

Jerry recently learned that the crews had used some of the stockpiled "storm inventory" without his permission. The lack of cooperation between departments was another indicator of the problems brewing between them. Jerry was beginning to think that William intentionally encouraged crews to be slack about record-keeping.

———————————————

Morgan entered the conference room. "Good afternoon, everybody," she said in the bubbly voice she used whenever she sensed tension in the air. "What's going on? What's wrong, you guys?"

Jerry turned to her, clenching his teeth. "William's on my back about Magnolia Road and some missing poles. My inventory records are a mess—how was I to know we were short? Ask *him* why his people haven't been following the rules and keeping a good accounting."

In a calming voice, Morgan asked if the two could work things out on their own.

Jerry shook his head and muttered, "He's too ambitious. He'll step on anybody to get ahead."

"I can't have you guys disagreeing like this!" Morgan responded.

It was William's turn. "Same excuses, same problem six months ago, when we had no relay switches in stock. Now it's power poles, and that's a hell of a lot worse."

Morgan got more direct. "Work out your differences. Listen to each other's opinions and viewpoints. Set a positive example for the rest of the organization."

A deafening silence consumed the room.

Morgan began to realize that central stores might indeed be hugely under-stocked. They would be in big trouble if a storm hit.

As if this internal problem wasn't enough, she might have to face the national media, which she had little respect for. She knew the drill: They would exploit the public's fear of storms by broadcasting frequent warnings and updates. Those media reports raised a community's anxiety and caused utilities across the region to scramble for limited equipment and supplies. Most times, there would be no storm, but tens of thousands of angry people.

Kitty made her way to the conference table. "Sorry I'm late." Being late seemed to be the rule rather than the exception, but Morgan understood Kitty's consistent tardiness. Kitty simply couldn't end her own meetings on time. All too often, she ended up helping an employee with a personal problem. Kitty loved this part of her new job—counseling and helping people. She especially loved it compared to being with Jerry and William.

Sensing the friction in the room, Kitty composed herself and tried to reduce the tension. "This argument seems awfully familiar. There must be some way to get beyond this stalemate." *Who wouldn't want to be late to a meeting like this?* she thought.

Both William and Jerry looked away from her.

Morgan read the mood of the people on her senior "team" and decided that the best way to defuse the situation was to start the meeting and announce its purpose: to prepare for the storm. "Guys, I know we have our plates full, but this time Mr. Brown isn't around to help us, may he rest in peace. You two are upset about what's going on between central stores and operations, and Kitty, you like conducting employee counseling sessions, but right now we have a bigger problem. That storm. It might be coming our way."

"That's just newscaster propaganda," Jerry retorted. "Those guys are selling advertising. They do it every hurricane season. It's their game. Communities get stirred up over nothing. The storm isn't going to be that bad. Remember, last year we got all worked up over Hurricane Edward and it missed us. So who's to say this one is coming our way? We shouldn't be bullied into joining the panic; this will end up being nothing more than another media event. Let's wait forty-eight hours before we use our precious time planning and taking crews away from their scheduled work. Hey, we've got enough problems just keeping the power on every day."

Jerry gave one more jab to William, adding, "Anyway, this planning is all sort of in vain, since we don't even have the materials on hand, thanks to William's crews and their spotty record keeping."

William couldn't keep quiet. "Jerry, that's so typical of you. Just because there hasn't been a direct hit in almost one hundred years, we still have to prepare for it!"

Morgan shook her head at him. "I believe Jerry's right. We have so many other things to worry about and get caught up on before we start planning for a storm that might pass us over like all the others."

"And if it doesn't? We're short of supplies—again—and our operations record keeping doesn't have—"

Morgan cut him off. "Folks, we can't have this. I need your help. We have got to work together. Let's take those forty-eight hours and cool off."

William said, "No, Morgan. I don't think we can wait two days. Someone needs to step up to the plate. Other utilities around us are planning; they're probably buying up all the supplies and materials *we* should be purchasing. We need to get moving. *We need a better storm plan.* What we have won't get us through a category four."

Morgan said, "So, what do you think, William?"

"I'm the operations engineer, so let me take this off your back. You've got enough going on, with the media playing up the severity of the storm, the mayors, and the panicky public. I'll develop a real disaster plan. Be assured, my operations department works 24/7, unlike a few other departments around this table. I can have it ready in two days. No need for worry."

A skeptical Jerry muttered to himself, "Plan, plan, plan. You can't even get your crews to record materials accurately in a log."

William shot back. "If you'd take the time to plan, we wouldn't be low on inventory."

Morgan spoke up again. "Folks, please stop this. We need to make a decision and get moving."

"No problem. I can handle it," responded William. "Here are the assignments. Kitty, you review all of the mutual aid plans we have with other utilities. Call them and make sure that they're on alert. It would be nice if we had a coordinator across the region to do this, but we don't, so you're just going to have to call them individually.

"Jerry, you need to get some pressure on those suppliers and make sure we have enough materials to rebuild thirty percent of the system, and that we have one hundred miles of conductor on hand. I'll come up with a game plan based on the worst-case scenario. We'll take care of everything for you here, Morgan, so you can be our public face in the community. I'm sure all those elected officials will be calling, not to mention those pesky reporters."

"That sounds great. Thanks so much, William. We'll meet again on Friday. That should give us plenty of time."

They adjourned as the storm moved closer and gained in intensity.

William walked briskly back to his office. The stage was set for the opportunity he had been dreaming about. With Morgan, a non-engineer in the lead seat, his star could shine.

He called a meeting with a few select employees, favorites in the operations group. He updated them on Jerry's chaos: lack of inventory for routine jobs and depleted storm materials. He whispered that the new "boss lady" wouldn't be riding in on a white horse to save the day, so it would be up to them to do so. He insisted that they work on a new operations plan with Friday's meeting in mind. The group discussed the impending storm and what they would have ready. Some of the employees got off track, daydreaming out loud about the heroes they would be within the utility and in the community for saving the day if this storm rolled ashore.

William dominated the meeting, as usual. He had assembled a group of "yes" men, and no one dared to challenge his ideas. William had always intimidated employees with his relentless drive. No one wanted to get steamrolled in the process. Each person wanted to keep a seat at his table.

After the operations meeting, William had a few discreet conversations with Jerry's employees. He hinted that Jerry should retire, because he was out of touch and couldn't handle preparations for a monster storm. He even refused to believe one was headed their way.

With his base of support extended to Jerry's key people, William made a critical decision to withhold a detailed materials plan for central stores. Consumed by his frustration with Jerry, it never occurred to him what this would do to his own operations group and the ultimate restoration of electric power to the community.

Rumors and speculation circulated throughout the utility about what was happening among the senior staff since Doug Brown's death. Employees sensed the escalating conflict between Jerry's and William's departments. The water cooler buzz was that the new boss lady wouldn't tolerate that kind of back-stabbing and that once hurricane season passed, there would be a shake-up at the top. Some employees criticized Jerry for having his head stuck in the sand, while others criticized William for having an inner circle of favorites.

Morgan returned to her office feeling less certain about her ability to manage the senior staff. She questioned herself and wondered if she had made the wrong decision to give William the responsibility to prepare the expanded storm plan, without first getting input from the others. Skeptical about his eagerness to take charge without involving Jerry and Kitty, she questioned William's motivation and worried that the growing conflict with Jerry might end up undermining the utility's overall effectiveness.

Convinced that William wanted to use the storm threat to his own advantage, Jerry decided to stick with the existing plan that had been created by Doug Brown. After all, it had worked well in the past, and Jerry did not want to be a pawn in William's quest to rise to the top. He'd recently heard a rumor that Morgan planned to create a new position for William. If true, William would be elevated to "group" department head, meaning that everyone else on senior staff, including him, would report to him directly.

Jerry knew that Morgan's promotion had been a mistake. *He* should have gotten the job, even if only for the duration of the hurricane season. A novice non-engineer at the top didn't make sense. She couldn't possibly understand the technical aspects of the job in such a short time frame. That poor decision to promote her, compounded by her own bad decision to over-react to this potential storm, could only lead to a future with dreadful management. And that meant a waste of budget dollars.

Friday

A Look at the Plan

By late Friday afternoon, the staff learned that the storm had moved to within a few days of their coastline. State officials announced a voluntary evacuation of the area, and a possible mandatory evacuation of the entire coastal region as the storm's projected path became more certain. This could be not only a natural disaster, but also a management disaster!

Morgan began the storm committee meeting as Kitty and Jerry sat quietly in anticipation of William's detailed plan to deal with a possible monster storm.

William started reviewing his plan. He gave detailed guidance on how his operations group would deploy extra personnel out in the field. Then he got to the other parts of the plan that dealt with Kitty's and Jerry's areas. That took him less than ten minutes to cover. Even with Morgan's limited technical knowledge, she knew that William had let the others down. He provided no direction regarding possible needs or priorities in any department other than his own. The plan did not contain any specific guidance regarding materials, supplies, or additional personnel.

Morgan was stunned. Her worst fear had come to pass.

"I can't believe this!" Jerry raised his voice. "Was this intentional? You promised us a written, detailed plan, but you've included nothing about my department or Kitty's. If you had told us that this was your idea of a plan, I could have started working on mine two days ago!"

"You didn't think there was a need for a new plan two days ago!" William retorted.

Morgan quickly took charge of the discussion. "Regardless of what has or has not happened in the last forty-eight hours, William, you need to get to work on the missing part of the plan, and *now*. No wasting time. Any conflicts will have to be worked out later."

Kitty and Jerry worked around the clock over the weekend to prepare the details of their responsibilities. The going was slow. Chaos had started across the community and region as the storm's track became more definite. Jerry cursed the vendors he couldn't reach.

Monday

The Storm Committee Meets Again

Morgan sat and tapped her fingers on the conference table. William wasn't on time for the storm committee meeting. Making storm plans for his crews came first, he explained when he finally called in. He promised to get back to the office as soon as possible.

Five hours later, William returned and Morgan sent word to Jerry and Kitty. Morgan called the meeting to order as soon as everyone settled in.

Kitty's pulse began to race as she felt a sickening contempt for William. *How could he have put off this important meeting for five long hours when he knew there was so much to be coordinated among the departments?* He cared so little for people's needs and feelings. *This man has ice in his veins!* She wanted to cry with frustration, but wouldn't give William the satisfaction—he would just call her weak. She put on her best face to show that she could handle tough times. She was not going to show confusion or fear.

Kitty took a deep breath and began her report. "I've reserved one hundred hotel rooms, and have enough food for five days," she said. "I've tried to reach sister utilities to execute the mutual aid plans to get additional workers, but only one of my phone calls has been returned."

Jerry frowned.

Kitty felt the tension building up inside of her. "This is not my fault! Why don't utilities have a single coordinator for a region? None of the existing plans even specify a contact person's name or even a job title. Everything is so out of date and uncoordinated here. I am an HR professional, not an electrical engineer!"

"Does this mean you don't have additional crews lined up to help?" Jerry demanded.

"Just a few," Kitty replied. "How do you expect me to execute a workforce plan that requires me to know what kind and how many technical workers to request from other utilities? What am I to do?"

Jerry wasn't surprised. He'd always questioned Kitty's lack of expertise. He couldn't figure out why Morgan had appointed her to the storm committee in the first place. She had no technical background or knowledge of electrical systems. She couldn't possibly communicate their needs effectively with the mutual aid utilities, even if she could get through to someone on the phone.

Morgan sensed from Jerry's expression that he wasn't finished with Kitty yet, so she defused the situation by asking William to report on his end. This time, William provided specific estimates on supplies and equipment needed to support the crews. Jerry thought the inventory estimates were excessive, and said so.

"Damn it, Jerry, we can't over-prepare for this storm!" William retorted.

Jerry reluctantly said that he'd do his best to get them, and Morgan ended the meeting feeling less than confident. "I guess we're ready," she said, but there was a note of doubt in her voice.

Jerry walked out of the building and thought about what had just transpired. *I don't care what William says he needs. We're already over budget for the year. His people won't complete our check-out forms, so why should I continue to cower at his last-minute demands? I'm not going to sit in the hot seat later this year for exceeding budget by ordering everything he says we'll need. All this panic will have been forgotten by then.*

In fact, Jerry had no intention of pushing to get the equipment and supplies. *I've been here thirty-five years, and I've weathered storms before,* he said to himself. *I'm not wasting a dime on materials we may not need, when William's guys are just going to abuse our inventory system again. I'd be criticized, and I'm not going out on retirement that way.*

He told his secretary about the meeting. "William is trying to make a name for himself. Look at these ridiculous estimates! He wants us to jump through hoops at the last minute because his folks didn't follow check-out procedures. He's going to try and make us look like fools!"

───────────────

Meanwhile, Kitty frantically placed calls to the mutual aid utilities. *She* would show *them* who was tough. She sensed what Jerry had been hinting at: that she was overwhelmed in the job. Her feelings were hurt, but she knew she and Jerry didn't have the same understanding about the importance of people and relationships in getting work done as a team. Of course, she'd never say this to his face. She'd always hidden her true feelings from him, because she wanted Jerry and everyone else to like her. Besides, Jerry cared only about productivity and telling people what to do—clear evidence that his leadership style was old-school and out of date.

Kitty re-focused and called a few more utilities. The lack of response was pretty discouraging. This "special storm" job responsibility didn't fit her very well. She preferred to help people face-to-face and disliked the technical aspects and coordination part of the job.

She hoped for the success of her trusted assistant, now a personal friend, to pull through with mutual aid contacts. Otherwise, the utility would be left without enough critical outside workers.

Chapter Three

Direct Hit

Tuesday

Morgan's worst nightmare had come true. At first, the storm had stalled off the coast for more than a day, becoming weaker. Then, early that morning, the storm was upgraded to a category-four hurricane, with sustained winds of almost 145 miles per hour. Their beautiful and historic city sat directly in the center of its projected path.

Morgan gathered in the dispatch center with Jerry, William, and Kitty to ride out the storm. Later in the day, it struck. The four silently monitored the wall display of the entire electrical system. One by one, they watched the lighted areas of the panels go black as the main lines of service went dead. Eventually, there was only darkness and the whining of the wind.

The howling storm struck the community head on. The eye of the hurricane passed directly over the downtown business area and their own operations center. In the halls, Morgan could hear some employees sobbing quietly. She knew they were desperate to be with their families during this time of destruction. She silently prayed for everyone's safety.

The senior staff waited together, physically isolated from the rest of the world for the next six hours. By the time the eye of the storm passed, all electricity was gone. There was no TV, no radio, and no cell phone service. Some telephone land lines remained, but they were jammed because people from all over the country were calling into the region to check on their loved ones.

Damage reports started trickling in via land line, confirming that the storm had ravaged this beautiful coastal community.

It was the strongest hurricane in almost a century, and it left the area in a jumbled mess of twisted trees, shattered homes, snapped utility poles, and mangled electric transmission lines. The trail of damage extended inland across half of the state. Ten deaths were reported along the coast and beyond. Devastated people roamed the streets in shock and disbelief. Families were separated, with no way to locate one another.

From an infrastructure standpoint, damage estimates would be astronomical—maybe well into the hundreds of millions of dollars. The size and force of the storm triggered events that would further complicate the utility's efforts to restore power. Most hotel rooms had been reserved by large national insurance companies coming in to assess the damage, leaving little available for out-of-area electric crews from mutual-aid utilities. The only connection to an island community, an antiquated drawbridge, collapsed into the water, and the utility had no barge necessary to bypass the bridge and transport heavy equipment there. The plane that the utility had rented in the past to survey transmission rights-of-way had been scooped up and leased to a national news crew. Gasoline shortages kept line trucks and bulldozers from moving into immediate action.

The list of complications went on and on.

Post-Storm Meeting

Morgan called a storm-committee meeting after the hurricane passed to assess the damage to the electrical system and get estimates of how quickly the power could be restored.

She walked into the conference room tired and frustrated from an earlier meeting with anxious elected officials and reporters, where she was subjected to a stream of questions about specific power restoration estimates from the county's head of emergency preparedness.

William had been out in the field conducting the assessment.

Kitty had been busy directing the few out-of-town crews to available hotels, and establishing feeding sites.

Jerry had been tracking down regional vendors.

In the dull glow of emergency lighting, they huddled together and listened to an exasperated William share his storm assessment.

Storm Assessment

My field lieutenants and storm assessors paint a grim picture of what the storm's fury has meant to the integrity of our electrical transmission and distribution system. Only one of our key transmission lines providing bulk power to the region remains standing and undamaged. Several other transmission lines have suffered major damage to wooden structures that are inaccessible to trucks and conventional line equipment. Unfortunately, these are the very lines that will require immediate attention, since they are integral to restoring service to the substations and distribution system.

Many of the major switching stations have also suffered water and wind damage to relay equipment and battery houses. Several substation transformer banks will require repair to key components, such as high voltage bushings and voltage regulators. Availability of replacement equipment is a major issue for the substation crews. Line supervisors are concerned about crews rushing in to make repairs without focusing on safe work practices, and everyone is feeling the pressure.

(continued)

The blaming started immediately. Kitty went first. "I am new
here, and William did not give me detailed directions on
recruiting and mobilizing personnel until it was too late."

"You're the HR person. You're in charge of people. Don't you
know how to mobilize people?" William charged Kitty. "Don't
you know how to make plans to house and feed people?"

"Please don't point the finger at me. I did the best I could.
Look at the information I had. I asked my assistant to help,
but she was just too busy. We couldn't make all those calls by
ourselves," Kitty said defensively.

Jerry chimed in. "I saw this coming. William, you didn't give
Kitty what she needed in that plan of yours. And Morgan,
sorry for saying this, but we needed for you to provide clear
direction. Instead, you made some rash decisions and passed
off your responsibility to William."

"None of you stepped up to the plate!" responded William.
"Now you blame *me*. Why didn't you come up with your own
details earlier? I had the plan for my department detailed.
The reason I'm having problems is that Jerry didn't get the
materials. We don't even have enough gasoline and diesel
fuel. Even if we had enough fuel, we still don't know where to
send the bulldozers, because the plane is leased out. And
Kitty, we won't have enough hotel rooms or food. We may
have to turn away some of the outside help."

Morgan shouted, "Whose job was it to see that we had a plane on standby for aerial surveillance?"

William looked straight at Jerry and said, "It wasn't my job. The last time I looked at a plane, it was a big piece of *e-quip-ment!*"

"It's somebody's fault," Morgan declared, "and somebody's head is going to roll, but it's not going to be mine. When I get back in a few hours, I want this straightened out once and for all."

Morgan headed back to the emergency center. Luckily, it was just down the street and she didn't have to travel far, because the roads were barely passable. She spent the next ten hours fending off questions from elected officials, who wanted specific answers about restoring power to hospitals, sewer pumps, and other critical operations. Police wanted power restored in the business areas to stop civil disobedience and looting. People were clearly in shock, and power was essential to calming them down and reducing their fears about safety.

Morgan left the center exhausted. She had no way to predict the return of power, and she couldn't even predict what would happen when she returned to the operations center.

A local newspaper reporter was sitting in the waiting area outside of her office when she got back. He wanted to verify reports that the utility did not have enough people and equipment on hand to restore power quickly, and she knew she had to give him some time.

After the interview, she took a deep breath as it all began to sink in. The real disaster had happened at the utility company *she* was responsible for, which was supposed to provide customers living in this beautiful coastal region with safe, reliable power. Soon more reporters, the community, and the entire country would know how they screwed up by not having enough people, equipment, and materials. She and the senior staff were unprepared, having gotten caught up in their own storms. And because they did not see those storms brewing, they created what would be a very difficult recovery effort.

Part II

Power Restoration

Chapter Four

Recovery

Morgan walked through the door of a local bookstore to meet her friend Karen for coffee, thinking about the past three months and the hundreds of TV interviews, news shows, newspaper articles, and stinging letters to the editor about the utility. She had been reviled by the community for mishandling the power restoration process. Feeling hurt and powerless, she was ashamed at the utility's failure to properly prepare for the storm. She felt so hurt and embarrassed, in fact, that she rarely went out in public. She disguised herself in a large, wide-brimmed baseball cap embossed with the state's logo as she got ready to meet Karen. Her normally coiffed hair was now straight and pulled back in a ponytail. Wearing jeans, she hardly resembled the executive manager of an electric utility.

Karen, the superintendent of public schools, would understand what it is like to be in the public eye and under such scrutiny. Who better to go to for consolation and advice?

Morgan relayed the whole story about Doug Brown's death, the storm's direct hit, and the slow storm recovery. She felt a lump build in her throat as she recalled the events.

Karen reached for her hand. "Morgan, you're upset—and that's natural. Remember, you did your best. It's time to acknowledge what happened, take new action, and avoid repeating the same mistakes. It hasn't been an easy road for me, either. Public schools are complicated, too. Let me show you a book that helped me as a leader when I was going through some tough times. This book has changed my life. It opened my eyes like never before. Let's see if they have it in stock."

Without another word, Morgan and Karen carried their coffees and headed to the other side of the bookstore. Karen scanned the shelves, reached for a book, and handed it to Morgan. Morgan read the title and turned to the introduction. She read the definition of polarities or interdependent pairs that "need" each other over time to gain and sustain higher performance. And she kept reading . . .

Chapter Five

Power Surge

Since we all don't have friends like Karen to lead us through difficult times, let me take this opportunity to explain how someone like Morgan can end up in this kind of circumstance—and manage it before it gets out of control, if not prevent it.

What you need is an understanding of interdependent values—two values that seem very different, and yet can be paired up to raise and sustain a higher level of leadership performance. These interdependent pairs of values are called "polarities," and I wrote this book to show you just how easily you can learn how to keep them in balance when you work with people.

Each person in this story has a different way of leading and interacting with others. Their actions are driven by a set of strong beliefs that guide how they think and what they do as a leader. Each person operates with some number of Motivational Values that, in their minds, equates to success as a leader. These Motivational Values represent what he or she believes is the "right way" to lead and work with others. Unfortunately, none of the staff members in the story had any understanding of related Interdependent Values. Consequently, their deeply held beliefs caused them to be less effective as individuals and within their team.

```
┌─────────────────────────────────────────────────────────┐
│                  What Is a Motivational Value?            │
│                                                           │
│  • It is an important quality or principle about yourself.│
│    (Dependability.)                                       │
│                                                           │
│  • It guides what you say or do.                          │
│    (I keep my commitments.)                               │
│                                                           │
│  • It represents a principle or standard that directs     │
│    your actions as a leader.                              │
│    (Others can rely on me as a leader to follow through,  │
│    because I'm known for my word being my bond.)          │
│                                                           │
└─────────────────────────────────────────────────────────┘
```

Understanding How Polarities Work

You will see the term "point of view" used several times in this section. I use it here to refer to the tendency we all have to see only one part of a polarity at a time. It is this half of the pair that we focus most of our energies on. The downside of this, however, is that the other value falls off our radar screen. We end up seeing only one half of the picture—not the whole picture—just one set of values with related fears. The other point of view that we don't see, and thus neglect, is our blind spot.

If I really only see one point of view (such as to value humility and to fear being too confident), I will probably come across as a leader who lacks confidence, and I will experience the negatives of being too humble.

It is important to recognize that all polarities reflect two points of view.

- Each point of view is correct, but the leader needs to tap both points of view in order to succeed over time.

- Each point of view is made up of a value and fear combination. For example, if I value being *dependable,* then I probably fear being a *slacker.*

- The stronger the emotional attachment to a value, the greater will be the fear of its loss.

If you plot out a values pair on what we call a Polarity Map, you will get a concrete and whole picture, rather than just your own single point of view. When you learn to identify a Motivational Value with its associated Interdependent Value, you heighten your ability to see complex circumstances in a simpler and yet broader vantage point.

Analysis of Morgan's Leadership

Morgan's ultimate goal (and the goal of many of you) is to be an effective leader. Humility is an important Motivational Value for her. She acts with great humility in leading others to achieve success at the utility. From Morgan's point of view, it's easy for her to see the positive results when she focuses on Humility, because she wants to:

- Appear unpretentious and approachable
- Seem easy to be around
- Demonstrate openness to others' ideas

Another motivating factor to keep Morgan focused on Humility is that she wants to avoid being seen as:

- Arrogant
- Difficult to be around
- Closed to others' ideas

These sorts of concerns cause her to believe even more strongly that humility is the "right way" for an effective leader to act. She consequently places greater and greater emphasis on Humility.

What Morgan hasn't realized is that her Motivational Value, Humility, can make her vulnerable over time because she doesn't see Humility as part of an interdependent pair. Since she can't recognize this, she fails to incorporate the other value of the interdependent pair into her actions as a leader. In Morgan's situation, Confidence is the Interdependent Value that is being neglected.

By neglecting Confidence, Morgan misses out on these positive results that could help her appear to:

- Look assured in her demeanor
- Set clear and predictable expectations
- Face the unknown as she moves forward to drive organizational results

So, by focusing solely on Humility to guide her actions as a leader—and neglecting Confidence over time—Morgan's strengths turn into weaknesses. Here are some negative results Morgan experiences at the utility because she over-focuses on Humility and neglects Confidence:

- She looks unsure.
- She sets unclear and unpredictable expectations.
- She retreats from the unknown (and so organizational results suffer).

With such an over-focus on her Motivational Value, Humility, Morgan is destined to under-perform.

At this point, you might be saying to yourself, *Sure, I can see that. It's obvious that Morgan needs to exhibit both Humility and Confidence in order to exert effective leadership.*

While this may seem obvious to you in your analysis of Morgan, it is most often because we can see in others what we can't see in ourselves.

In fact, the more strongly we embrace our Motivational Values and believe that we are saying and doing the "right" things, the more difficult it is for us to recognize that an Interdependent Value exists. Again, I think of this as a blind spot.

I've found that it is much easier to identify the missing part of the interdependent pair using a Polarity Map. It makes visible and concrete what is either somewhat intuitive or is oftentimes completely out of our realm of possibility. Polarity Mapping helps a leader shine light on the blind spot and see the larger, whole picture. By identifying what is needed to create and sustain higher performance, the leader's viewpoint is expanded and enhanced.

This awareness has helped me and countless others raise our consciousness to be more effective as leaders and more effective in life in general.

Polarity Management Mapping Objectives

You will have a better idea of what it takes to be an effective leader if you do these six things:

Six Steps to Leadership Effectiveness Using Polarities

1. Identify your key Motivational Values.
2. Find an Interdependent Value to supplement each Motivational Value.
3. View both values as a working pair to be managed and balanced over time.
4. Put them on a Polarity Map, so you can see the positive results and the potential negative results from both values.
5. Create a plan to achieve and maintain higher performance, thereby tapping into the pair's synergy.
6. Recognize early on when you are out of balance, so that you can take corrective action.

Polarity Management Map

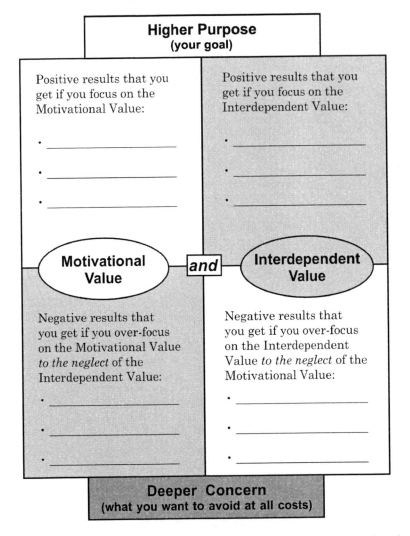

A Polarity Map provides the "container" for the pair of values. There is a box at the top and a box at the bottom of the map, along with four quadrants that illustrate the positive results from each value and the negative results you can get if you over-focus on one to the neglect of the other. The diagonal shading in the four quadrants amplifies that the pair of values produces results that are polar opposites.

How to Read a Polarity Management Map *(concluded)*

Values: The ovals contain the interdependent pair of values you need to incorporate over time in order to achieve higher performance and sustain it.

Higher Purpose: The box at the top is called the "Higher Purpose" statement. It answers this question: Ultimately, what am I trying to achieve? That is, what is my goal?

Deeper Concern: The box at the bottom is called the "Deeper Concern." It is always the opposite of the Higher Purpose statement. The Deeper Concern is what you really want to avoid at all costs.

Interdependence: The *"and"* box in the middle is a reminder that the two values are interdependent. Therefore, the connection is *"and,"* rather than *"either/or."*

Results: Four quadrants show the positive results from each value and the negative results you can get if you neglect the other value in the pair over time.

Polar Opposites: While the values are interdependent, the results from them are polar opposites. They are represented in the four quadrants by shaded diagonals.

How to Fill out a Polarity Map

Drawing a Polarity Map is easy if you do one part at a time. Let's begin with a Motivational Value in Morgan's example.

Points of View

Morgan's leadership is rooted in her Motivational Value: *Humility.* This strong belief guides her in what is the "right" way for an effective leader to act. When she thinks of Humility, she holds a point of view with two parts: the positive results she associates with Humility, and the negative results she associates with a leader who lacks Humility (the results she wants to avoid). So her point of view looks like this:

Motivational Value Point of View

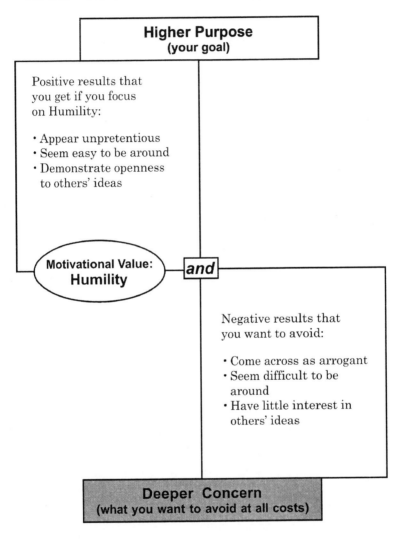

Higher Purpose
(your goal)

Positive results that
you get if you focus
on Humility:

• Appear unpretentious
• Seem easy to be around
• Demonstrate openness
  to others' ideas

Motivational Value:
Humility

and

Negative results that
you want to avoid:

• Come across as arrogant
• Seem difficult to be
  around
• Have little interest in
  others' ideas

Deeper Concern
(what you want to avoid at all costs)

Now let's look at the second part, starting with the other half of the Interdependent Pair: Confidence.

This second viewpoint Morgan can't see for herself. Because she so deeply believes in Humility, she fails to see the importance of also having Confidence, the other half of the Interdependent Values pair. Without seeing this, Morgan is unable to recognize that she needs a very different set of positive results if she is to be more effective. Finally, Morgan can't imagine that she could, in fact, experience some negative results if she over-focuses on Humility and neglects Confidence.

Missing Point of View

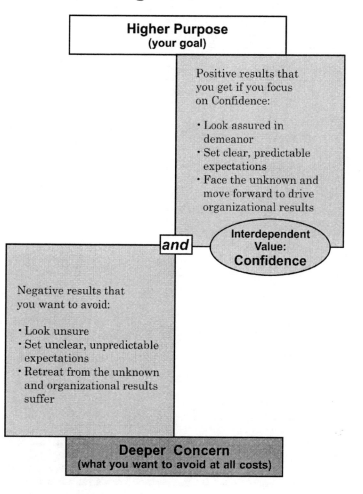

Higher Purpose
(your goal)

Positive results that you get if you focus on Confidence:

• Look assured in demeanor
• Set clear, predictable expectations
• Face the unknown and move forward to drive organizational results

and

Interdependent Value: Confidence

Negative results that you want to avoid:

• Look unsure
• Set unclear, unpredictable expectations
• Retreat from the unknown and organizational results suffer

Deeper Concern
(what you want to avoid at all costs)

The power of the *"and"* lies in Morgan's ability to see both points of view simultaneously. Plotting these on a Polarity Map makes it easier for her to see both points of view, and helps her reach that awareness easily.

Understanding her Motivational Value (Humility) and the Interdependent Value (Confidence) by mapping the working pair, Morgan is able to view her leadership from a broader perspective. The map represents the whole picture; it is an expanded view of effective leadership, which consists of both points of view.

Polarity Management Map

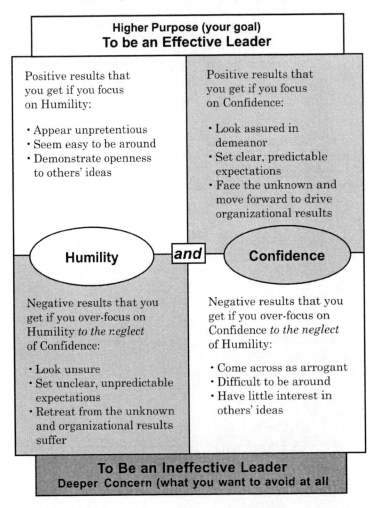

Higher Purpose (your goal)
To be an Effective Leader

Positive results that you get if you focus on Humility:

- Appear unpretentious
- Seem easy to be around
- Demonstrate openness to others' ideas

Positive results that you get if you focus on Confidence:

- Look assured in demeanor
- Set clear, predictable expectations
- Face the unknown and move forward to drive organizational results

Humility *and* **Confidence**

Negative results that you get if you over-focus on Humility *to the neglect* of Confidence:

- Look unsure
- Set unclear, unpredictable expectations
- Retreat from the unknown and organizational results suffer

Negative results that you get if you over-focus on Confidence *to the neglect* of Humility:

- Come across as arrogant
- Difficult to be around
- Have little interest in others' ideas

To Be an Ineffective Leader
Deeper Concern (what you want to avoid at all

The Infinity Loop

The Infinity Loop is a graphic design used here to demonstrate the energy field in which the values pair exists. It shows their connectedness, as well as the ongoing movement between a Motivational Value and its Interdependent Value.

Once you have the whole picture of the importance of the values pair, the next step is to understand the importance of keeping the two values in balance over time. Since the two values are interdependent, they are thus connected, and must have each other forever. To neglect or abandon one or the other will cause a loss of performance at some point.

Also, you want to recognize that the relationship between the values pair is dynamic—not static. An effective leader is always shifting his or her focus from one value in the pair to the other, depending on changing needs and situations.

If you are chairing a series of meetings, for example, and you get the feeling that you are looking like you are unsure of yourself, you may need to shift to being more confident in expressing your expectations more clearly. Your goal is to be able to draw on the advantages of each value in the pair—to *not* focus on one to the neglect of the other.

Caution: It is crucial that you don't set an improvement goal to create a solitary focus on your newly-identified Interdependent Value, because you will inevitably neglect your own Motivational Value and experience a new set of problems. The key here is balance.

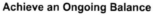

Achieve an Ongoing Balance

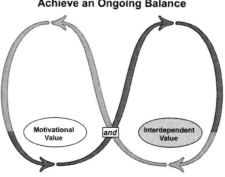

Motivational Value — and — Interdependent Value

Here's what Morgan's map looks like with the Infinity Loop.

Notice the location of the loop: it sits high in each of the four quadrants it passes through, signifying that the leader has done a highly effective job in achieving the positive results of both values, while minimizing the problems from neglecting either value. This is the most advantageous state of performance, and this is what Morgan hopes to achieve.

Ongoing Balance

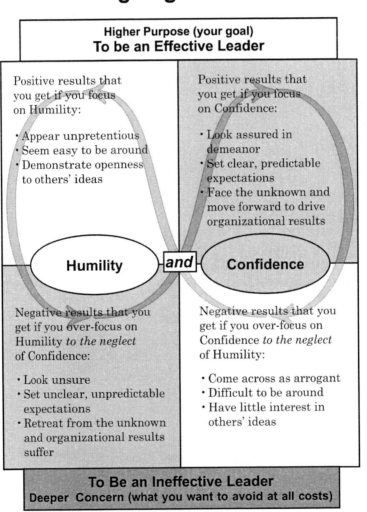

Higher Purpose (your goal)
To be an Effective Leader

Positive results that you get if you focus on Humility:

· Appear unpretentious
· Seem easy to be around
· Demonstrate openness to others' ideas

Positive results that you get if you focus on Confidence:

· Look assured in demeanor
· Set clear, predictable expectations
· Face the unknown and move forward to drive organizational results

Humility and **Confidence**

Negative results that you get if you over-focus on Humility *to the neglect* of Confidence:

· Look unsure
· Set unclear, unpredictable expectations
· Retreat from the unknown and organizational results suffer

Negative results that you get if you over-focus on Confidence *to the neglect* of Humility:

· Come across as arrogant
· Difficult to be around
· Have little interest in others' ideas

To Be an Ineffective Leader
Deeper Concern (what you want to avoid at all costs)

The final key element on the Polarity Map is a set of arrows that spiral up and down the center of the map. The arrows represent the potential positive results (synergy) or the potential negative results (problems) that are created by the leader's ability or inability to balance the values pair over time.

"Virtuous" Cycles and "Vicious" Cycles

Virtuous Cycles and Vicious Cycles are formed by a series of mutually reinforcing events that occur over time. They can be either positive or negative.

A Virtuous Cycle is a situation in which a favorable circumstance or result gives rise to another favorable circumstance that subsequently supports the first.

Conversely, a Vicious Cycle is a situation where the apparent solution to one problem creates a new problem OR increases the difficulty of solving the original problem.

Virtuous Cycles are created when the values pair works together to attain a Higher Purpose. The upward spiraling arrows point to the true power of the *"and."* It stands for **the potential positive gain that can be realized when you maintain a balance between the values pair over time.** That gain is called "synergy." As you consistently tap the positive results of each value in the pair, you increase your ability and capacity to achieve greater levels of performance. Performance is enhanced beyond what is capable when a leader has a sole point of view based only on one Motivational Value.

For example, Morgan can create Virtuous Cycles by supplementing her "easy to be around" demeanor with the "setting of clear and predictable expectations," because she will set them in a really nice and even way that is easy for people to accept.

Vicious Cycles can also be produced. The downward spiraling arrow illustrates **the negative results and reduced performance a leader can experience if one value is out of balance over time.**

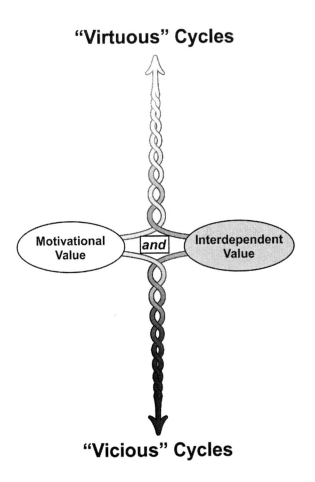

"Virtuous" Cycles

Motivational Value *and* **Interdependent Value**

"Vicious" Cycles

For example, if Morgan tries harder and harder to be more self-effacing and humble, she will continue to lose ground with her employees because she is showing a lack of confidence and direction. She will find herself trapped and moving toward total ineffectiveness as a leader. That is something every leader wants to avoid at all costs.

Here is Morgan's map again. It now includes arrows spiraling up and down, which reminds her that the goal is to create synergy so she can move upward toward her Higher Purpose, rather than downward toward her Deeper Concern.

Synergy to Achieve a Higher Purpose

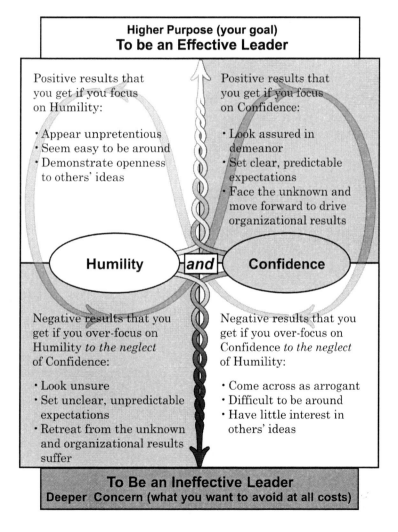

Higher Purpose (your goal)
To be an Effective Leader

Positive results that you get if you focus on Humility:

- Appear unpretentious
- Seem easy to be around
- Demonstrate openness to others' ideas

Positive results that you get if you focus on Confidence:

- Look assured in demeanor
- Set clear, predictable expectations
- Face the unknown and move forward to drive organizational results

Humility and **Confidence**

Negative results that you get if you over-focus on Humility *to the neglect* of Confidence:

- Look unsure
- Set unclear, unpredictable expectations
- Retreat from the unknown and organizational results suffer

Negative results that you get if you over-focus on Confidence *to the neglect* of Humility:

- Come across as arrogant
- Difficult to be around
- Have little interest in others' ideas

To Be an Ineffective Leader
Deeper Concern (what you want to avoid at all costs)

"Action Steps" and "Early Warnings"

Intentional Management of the Values Pair
Using the *"and"* Perspective

With heightened awareness and recognition of the significance of each value in the pair, Morgan is now ready to put her knowledge to work.

Action Steps

Action Steps are specific actions you can take to gain and/or maintain the positive results from a Motivational Value and its Interdependent Value. Since you are already doing some things that give you positive results, you should **record them and continue doing them.** Generally, you will need some new action steps to gain the positive results from the Interdependent Value, because it's what has been missing.

Caution: It is important to acknowledge the things you do currently as a leader that already serve you well. The new steps are to supplement what you've already mastered. Be careful not to stop doing what works, and don't ignore those things while you're working on the other half of the values pair. (You could lose the positive results you've gotten to date from your own Motivational Value.)

If Morgan stopped those actions associated with Humility, she might come across as arrogant.

Early Warnings

Early Warnings are measurable indicators (things you can see or count) that will let you know that you are getting negative results (the downside) of Humility or Confidence. Think about those indicators that would serve as early signals to you that you are over-focusing on one value to the neglect of the other.

Here are the Action Steps and Early Warnings that Morgan uses to gain and maintain an ongoing balance between Humility *and* Confidence:

Intentional Management of a Polarity Over Time

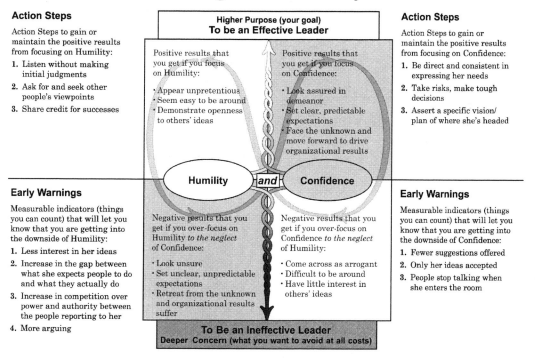

Action Steps

Action Steps to gain or maintain the positive results from focusing on Humility:

1. Listen without making initial judgments
2. Ask for and seek other people's viewpoints
3. Share credit for successes

Higher Purpose (your goal)
To be an Effective Leader

Positive results that you get if you focus on Humility:

· Appear unpretentious
· Seem easy to be around
· Demonstrate openness to others' ideas

Positive results that you get if you focus on Confidence:

· Look assured in demeanor
· Set clear, predictable expectations
· Face the unknown and move forward to drive organizational results

Humility *and* **Confidence**

Action Steps

Action Steps to gain or maintain the positive results from focusing on Confidence:

1. Be direct and consistent in expressing her needs
2. Take risks, make tough decisions
3. Assert a specific vision/plan of where she's headed

Early Warnings

Measurable indicators (things you can count) that will let you know that you are getting into the downside of Humility:

1. Less interest in her ideas
2. Increase in the gap between what she expects people to do and what they actually do
3. Increase in competition over power and authority between the people reporting to her
4. More arguing

Negative results that you get if you over-focus on Humility *to the neglect* of Confidence:

· Look unsure
· Set unclear, unpredictable expectations
· Retreat from the unknown and organizational results suffer

Negative results that you get if you over-focus on Confidence *to the neglect* of Humility:

· Come across as arrogant
· Difficult to be around
· Have little interest in others' ideas

Early Warnings

Measurable indicators (things you can count) that will let you know that you are getting into the downside of Confidence:

1. Fewer suggestions offered
2. Only her ideas accepted
3. People stop talking when she enters the room

To Be an Ineffective Leader
Deeper Concern (what you want to avoid at all costs)

High Performance: If the individual balances the values pair well, the infinity loop will reflect that synergy on the map. Most of the loop will be on the upper part of the map because most of the results will be positive. Only a small part of the loop will appear in the bottom part (negative results). This configuration illustrates the goal of the effective leader, who knows early on when and how to shift the focus in order to stay in balance and thus remain effective.

Successful balance over time demonstrates awareness, adaptability, and agility.

Polarity Map Template
Intentional Management of a Polarity Over Time

Action Steps

Action Steps to gain or maintain the positive results from focusing on the Motivational Value:

Action Steps

Action Steps to gain or maintain the positive results from focusing on the Interdependent Value:

Higher Purpose (your goal)
To be an Effective Leader

Positive results that you get if you focus on the Motivational Value:

Positive results that you get if you focus on the Interdependent Value:

Motivational Value *and* **Interdependent Value**

Early Warnings

Measurable indicators (things you can count) that will let you know that you are getting into the downside of the Motivational Value:

Early Warnings

Measurable indicators (things you can count) that will let you know that you are getting into the downside of the Interdependent Value:

Negative results that you get if you over-focus on the Motivational Value *to the neglect* of the Interdependent Value:

Negative results that you get if you over-focus on the Interdependent Value *to the neglect* of the Motivational Value:

To Be an Ineffective Leader
Deeper Concern (what you want to avoid at all costs)

Part III

Powerful Leading and Living

Chapter Six

Leaders in the Storm

Become a Coach to Morgan, Kitty, Jerry, and William

Now that you've seen how I coached Morgan to improve her performance by balancing Humility *and* Confidence, I want you to have an opportunity to coach her and the other senior staff at the utility. Keep in mind that these are all well-intentioned, hard-working people. They might even remind you of others you know. Maybe you will notice similarities in yourself during times of stress.

When you start to understand how natural strengths based on your Motivational Values can be supplemented to raise your performance as a leader, you will have taken a giant step toward lasting growth and development.

The following pages contain exercises that will test your learning. As you coach Morgan, Kitty, Jerry, and William, use the exercises to help you build Polarity Mapping skills. You will use these skills to look at your own leadership in Chapter Eight.

Sample Polarity Map for Morgan

Morgan Hendrix: Executive Manager

Morgan's problems and opportunities surrounding her leadership performance became clear once she learned to use a Polarity Map. She no longer had to rely solely on intuition and guessing in order to assess how well she is performing as a leader. This is one of the major reasons why more people are adopting the Polarity Management technique: it forces us to look at what is really happening.

Motivational Value for Morgan: Humility

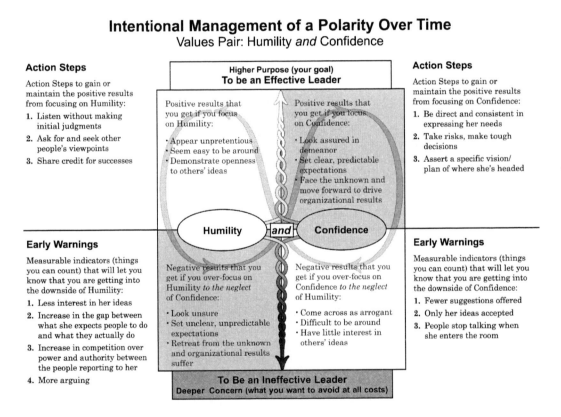

Intentional Management of a Polarity Over Time
Values Pair: Humility *and* Confidence

Action Steps

Action Steps to gain or maintain the positive results from focusing on Humility:

1. Listen without making initial judgments
2. Ask for and seek other people's viewpoints
3. Share credit for successes

Higher Purpose (your goal)
To be an Effective Leader

Positive results that you get if you focus on Humility:

· Appear unpretentious
· Seem easy to be around
· Demonstrate openness to others' ideas

Positive results that you get if you focus on Confidence:

· Look assured in demeanor
· Set clear, predictable expectations
· Face the unknown and move forward to drive organizational results

Action Steps

Action Steps to gain or maintain the positive results from focusing on Confidence:

1. Be direct and consistent in expressing her needs
2. Take risks, make tough decisions
3. Assert a specific vision/ plan of where she's headed

Humility *and* **Confidence**

Early Warnings

Measurable indicators (things you can count) that will let you know that you are getting into the downside of Humility:

1. Less interest in her ideas
2. Increase in the gap between what she expects people to do and what they actually do
3. Increase in competition over power and authority between the people reporting to her
4. More arguing

Negative results that you get if you over-focus on Humility *to the neglect* of Confidence:

· Look unsure
· Set unclear, unpredictable expectations
· Retreat from the unknown and organizational results suffer

Negative results that you get if you over-focus on Confidence *to the neglect* of Humility:

· Come across as arrogant
· Difficult to be around
· Have little interest in others' ideas

Early Warnings

Measurable indicators (things you can count) that will let you know that you are getting into the downside of Confidence:

1. Fewer suggestions offered
2. Only her ideas accepted
3. People stop talking when she enters the room

To Be an Ineffective Leader
Deeper Concern (what you want to avoid at all costs)

Morgan first looked at both sets of Early Warnings on the Polarity Map. She quickly determined that she was well out of balance in the days leading up to the storm.

She did not pick up on several Early Warnings that would have told her that she was over-focusing on Humility to the neglect of Confidence:

1. *Less interest in her ideas*
2. *Increase in the gap between what she expects people to do and what they actually do*
3. *Increase in competition over power and authority between the people reporting to her*
4. *More arguing*

On the other hand, she didn't see any signs or Early Warnings that she was over-focusing on Confidence to the neglect of Humility, such as:

1. *Fewer suggestions offered*
2. *Only her ideas accepted*
3. *People stop talking when she enters the room*

Based on her assessment of the Early Warnings, Morgan realized that her fear of being seen as arrogant was actually unfounded, because she displayed a consistent level of openness and modesty.

However, she clearly saw a need to place more emphasis on Confidence, so she decided to implement several Action Steps.

Morgan's Action Steps to increase her focus on Confidence:

1. *Be direct and consistent in expressing her needs*
2. *Take risks, make tough decisions*
3. *Assert a specific vision/plan of where she's headed*

Importantly, Morgan continued to carry out those Action Steps that had served her well in the past, which supported her Humility:

1. *Listen without making initial judgments*
2. *Ask for and seek other people's viewpoints*
3. *Share credit for successes*

Morgan wanted to be open and transparent with her employees about the reasons why she was changing her leadership style. She did not want employees becoming suspicious or distrustful when they saw her doing things differently. So, before Morgan took any new Action Steps associated with Confidence, she met individually with several key employees to share in general terms what she had learned about herself as a leader, and to alert them to specific changes they might notice regarding her leadership.

In the weeks and months that followed, Morgan periodically asked those same key employees for feedback so that she could determine the impact of her changes in leadership based on the Action Steps she had implemented. This was critical to her ongoing improvement.

Mapping Exercise #1

The best way for you to understand how to use polarities in your leadership life is to try a few exercises yourself. Let's start by looking more closely at Morgan's situation. How would you coach her to improve her leadership performance? Let's start by looking at this Polarity Map for one inter-dependent pair of values.

Motivational Value for Morgan: Listening to Others

Values Pair: Listening to Others *and* Expressing Own Views
Intentional Management of a Polarity Over Time

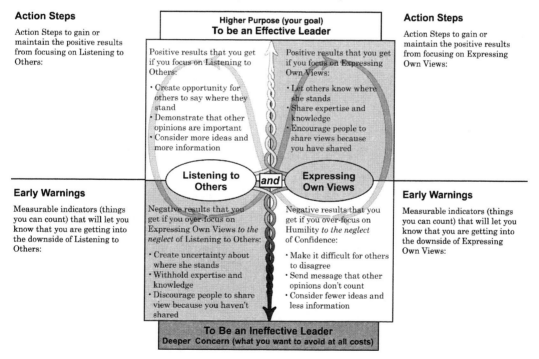

Action Steps

Action Steps to gain or maintain the positive results from focusing on Listening to Others:

Higher Purpose (your goal)
To be an Effective Leader

Positive results that you get if you focus on Listening to Others:

• Create opportunity for others to say where they stand
• Demonstrate that other opinions are important
• Consider more ideas and more information

Positive results that you get if you focus on Expressing Own Views:

• Let others know where she stands
• Share expertise and knowledge
• Encourage people to share views because you have shared

Action Steps

Action Steps to gain or maintain the positive results from focusing on Expressing Own Views:

Listening to Others — and — **Expressing Own Views**

Early Warnings

Measurable indicators (things you can count) that will let you know that you are getting into the downside of Listening to Others:

Negative results that you get if you over-focus on Expressing Own Views *to the neglect* of Listening to Others:

• Create uncertainty about where she stands
• Withhold expertise and knowledge
• Discourage people to share view because you haven't shared

Negative results that you get if you over-focus on Humility *to the neglect* of Confidence:

• Make it difficult for others to disagree
• Send message that other opinions don't count
• Consider fewer ideas and less information

Early Warnings

Measurable indicators (things you can count) that will let you know that you are getting into the downside of Expressing Own Views:

To Be an Ineffective Leader
Deeper Concern (what you want to avoid at all costs)

- Name two Action Steps you would suggest Morgan take that would produce the positive results listed on the map for the Motivational Value *Listening to Others*.

  _____

  _____

- Name two Action Steps you would suggest Morgan take that would produce the positive results listed on the map for the Interdependent Value *Expressing Own Views*.

  _____

  _____

- Provide two Early Warnings that would alert Morgan that she is over-focusing on *Listening to Others* to the neglect of *Expressing Her Own Views,* and that this is becoming a problem (Early Warnings = measurable, observable indicators).

  _____

  _____

- Provide two Early Warnings that would alert Morgan that she over-focusing on *Expressing her Own Views* to the neglect of *Listening to Others,* and that this is becoming a problem (Early Warnings = measurable, observable indicators).

  _____

  _____

Values Pair: **Swift Decision Making** *and* **Informed Decision Making**
Intentional Management of a Polarity Over Time

Action Steps

Action Steps to gain
or maintain the positive
results from focusing on
Swift Decision Making:

Action Steps

Action Steps to gain
or maintain the positive
results from focusing on
Informed Decision Making:

Higher Purpose (your goal)
To be an Effective Leader

Positive results that
you get if you focus on
Swift Decision Making:

• Cut through competing
 needs and information
 quickly
• Decide without all the facts
• Seize opportunities

Positive results that
you get if you focus on
Informed Decision Making:

• Analyze before taking
 action
• Create well-thought-out
 plans
• Reflect when needed

Swift Decision Making *and* **Informed Decision Making**

Early Warnings

Measurable indicators
(things you can count)
that will let you know
that you are getting
into the downside of
Swift Decision Making:

Early Warnings

Measurable indicators
(things you can count)
that will let you know
that you are getting
into the downside of
Informed Decision Making:

Negative results that you
get if you over-focus on
Swift Decision Making
to the neglect of Informed
Decision Making:

• Rush to action without
 analysis
• "Shoot from the hip"
 without planning
• React, unable to reflect

Negative results that you
get if you over-focus on
Informed Decision Making
to the neglect of Swift
Decision Making:

• Get "analysis paralysis"
• Put off decisions until
 all the facts are in
• Miss opportunities

To Be an Ineffective Leader
Deeper Concern (what you want to avoid at all costs)

- Name two Action Steps you would suggest Morgan take that would produce the positive results listed on the map for the Motivational Value *Swift Decision Making*.

_____

_____

- Name two Action Steps you would suggest Morgan take that would produce the positive results listed on the map for the Interdependent Value *Informed Decision Making*.

_____

_____

- Provide two Early Warnings that would alert Morgan that she is over-focusing on *Swift Decision Making* to the neglect of *Informed Decision Making,* and that this is becoming a problem (Early Warnings = measurable, observable indicators).

_____

_____

- Provide two Early Warnings that would alert Morgan that she is over-focusing on *Informed Decision Making* to the neglect of *Swift Decision Making,* and that this is becoming a problem (Early Warnings = measurable, observable indicators).

_____

_____

When completing this last map, Morgan realized something else. She learned that not only can strengths sometimes become weaknesses, but that Motivational Values can also lead to conflict between people. She now thought that the conflict between Jerry and William was really about differing values.

Also, Morgan recalled convincing Doug Brown to transfer a young engineer out of her department. The guy had really gotten under her skin. He was the type who kept dragging his feet. When it came to making decisions, he had to wait for every single ounce of information to be presented. His slow and methodical manner had made Morgan feel anxious and impatient. She eventually concluded that he was incompetent and unable to handle the demands of his job, so she gave him a poor performance review and eventually transferred him.

She now regretted taking this action. *This young man was motivated to help me make an informed decision, which was just what I needed in terms of leading my team,* she thought to herself. *He was someone who wouldn't have let me jump off the cliff. He would have helped us make a thorough storm plan and preparations.* She now understood the contributions he could have made.

Mapping Exercise #2:
Kitty Lanier, Director of Human Resources

Kitty has much to learn, because she struggled in her new position as HR director.

Complete this entire Polarity Map to clarify your understanding of what Kitty experienced, what she could learn from her struggles, and how you might coach her to improve her performance.

Motivational Value for Kitty: Relationships

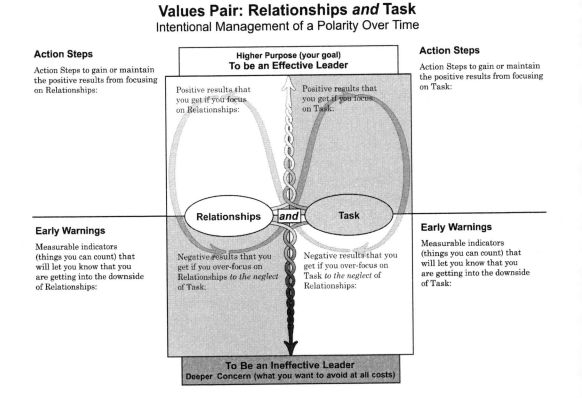

Values Pair: Relationships *and* Task
Intentional Management of a Polarity Over Time

Action Steps

Action Steps to gain or maintain the positive results from focusing on Relationships:

Higher Purpose (your goal)
To be an Effective Leader

Positive results that you get if you focus on Relationships:

Positive results that you get if you focus on Task:

Action Steps

Action Steps to gain or maintain the positive results from focusing on Task:

Relationships *and* Task

Early Warnings

Measurable indicators (things you can count) that will let you know that you are getting into the downside of Relationships:

Negative results that you get if you over-focus on Relationships *to the neglect* of Task:

Negative results that you get if you over-focus on Task *to the neglect* of Relationships:

Early Warnings

Measurable indicators (things you can count) that will let you know that you are getting into the downside of Task:

To Be an Ineffective Leader
Deeper Concern (what you want to avoid at all costs)

- What are two positive results Kitty got by focusing on her Motivational Value *Relationships*?

  _____

  _____

- What are two positive results Kitty could gain by focusing on the Interdependent Value *Task*?

  _____

  _____

- What are two negative results Kitty experienced because she over-focused on *Relationships* to the neglect of *Task*?

  _____

  _____

- What are two negative results Kitty would want to avoid from over-focusing on *Task* to the neglect of *Relationships*?

  _____

  _____

- What two Action Steps would you suggest Kitty take to get the positive results you've listed for her Motivational Value *Relationships*?

  _____

  _____

- What two Action Steps would you suggest Kitty take to produce the positive results you've listed for the Interdependent Value *Task?*

_____

_____

- Write down two Early Warnings that point to Kitty getting negative results because she has over-focused on *Relationships* to the neglect of *Task* (Early Warnings = measurable, observable indicators).

_____

_____

- Write down two Early Warnings that point to Kitty getting negative results because she has over-focused on *Task* to the neglect of *Relationships* (Early Warnings = measurable, observable indicators).

_____

_____

Mapping Exercise #3: Jerry Manigault, Director of Facilities and Central Stores

Even old-timers like Jerry want to be the best they can be. They're often concerned about legacy.

Complete this Polarity Map to illustrate your understanding of what Jerry learned and how you might coach him to improve his performance.

Motivational Value for Jerry: Candor

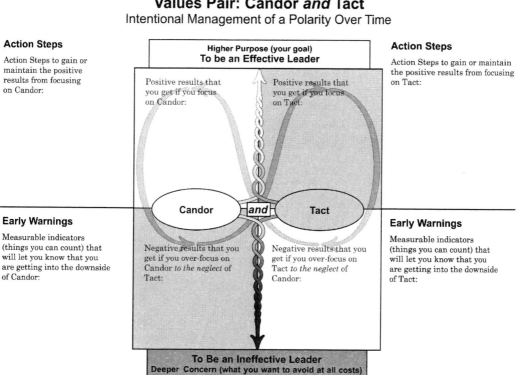

Values Pair: Candor *and* Tact
Intentional Management of a Polarity Over Time

Action Steps

Action Steps to gain or maintain the positive results from focusing on Candor:

Action Steps

Action Steps to gain or maintain the positive results from focusing on Tact:

Higher Purpose (your goal)
To be an Effective Leader

Positive results that you get if you focus on Candor:

Positive results that you get if you focus on Tact:

Candor *and* Tact

Early Warnings

Measurable indicators (things you can count) that will let you know that you are getting into the downside of Candor:

Negative results that you get if you over-focus on Candor *to the neglect* of Tact:

Negative results that you get if you over-focus on Tact *to the neglect* of Candor:

Early Warnings

Measurable indicators (things you can count) that will let you know that you are getting into the downside of Tact:

To Be an Ineffective Leader
Deeper Concern (what you want to avoid at all costs)

- What are two positive results Jerry got from his Motivational Value *Candor*?

_____

_____

- What are two positive results Jerry could gain by focusing on the Interdependent Value *Tact?*

_____

_____

- What are two negative results Jerry experienced because he over-focused on *Candor* to the neglect of *Tact*?

_____

_____

- What are two negative results Jerry would want to avoid from over-focusing on *Tact* to the neglect of *Candor*?

_____

_____

- What two Action Steps would you suggest Jerry take to get the positive results you've listed for his Motivational Value *Candor*?

_____

_____

- What two Action Steps would you suggest Jerry take to produce the positive results you've listed for the Inter-dependent Value *Tact*?

  _____

  _____

- Write down two Early Warnings that point to Jerry getting negative results because he has over-focused on *Candor* to the neglect of *Tact* (Early Warnings = measurable, observable indicators).

  _____

  _____

- Write down two Early Warnings that point to Jerry getting negative results because he has over-focused on *Tact* to the neglect of *Candor* (Early Warnings = measurable, observable indicators).

  _____

  _____

Mapping Exercise #4:
William Pringle, Former Director of Operations

Several days after the storm, William resigned from the utility, leaving before Morgan understood the reasons behind the team's terrible performance. In their final conversation, William repeated his strong belief that all good leaders look out for their own departments, first and foremost.

The objective of this mapping exercise is to show you how polarities exist at the organizational level, too. Complete the map about William's focus on his own department to the neglect of the whole organization.

Motivational Value for William: My Department

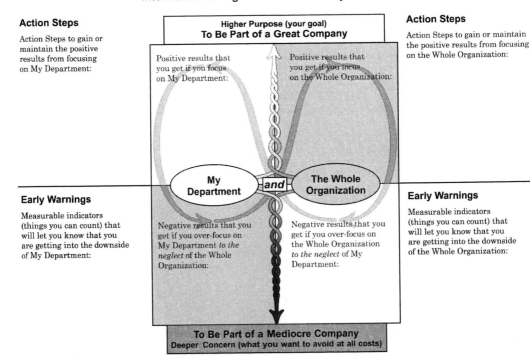

Values Pair: My Department *and* the Whole Organization
Intentional Management of a Polarity Over Time

Action Steps

Action Steps to gain or maintain the positive results from focusing on My Department:

Higher Purpose (your goal)
To Be Part of a Great Company

Positive results that you get if you focus on My Department:

Positive results that you get if you focus on the Whole Organization:

Action Steps

Action Steps to gain or maintain the positive results from focusing on the Whole Organization:

My Department *and* **The Whole Organization**

Early Warnings

Measurable indicators (things you can count) that will let you know that you are getting into the downside of My Department:

Negative results that you get if you over-focus on My Department *to the neglect* of the Whole Organization:

Negative results that you get if you over-focus on the Whole Organization *to the neglect* of My Department:

Early Warnings

Measurable indicators (things you can count) that will let you know that you are getting into the downside of the Whole Organization:

To Be Part of a Mediocre Company
Deeper Concern (what you want to avoid at all costs)

Learning from Experience

To conclude our story, Morgan reminded Kitty and Jerry about William's resignation. "This was a loss for both our team and the utility, and we need to forge ahead with a clean slate. It's important for the remaining three of us to talk about two values our team needs to move forward: Fairness *and* Forgiveness. I realize William let us down when we really were depending on him. Then, he resigned and left us to repair the damage within the utility and the damage to the community.

"I have an enormous request for both of you. I don't want us to spend our time and energy holding any resentment toward William. I want us to realize that he was leading based on his own strong belief that putting his department first and foremost was the "right" thing to do.

"Let's learn from this experience by honoring both Fairness *and* Forgiveness. Forgiveness is our opportunity to be compassionate and to release William from blame. If we don't forgive him, we'll just get stuck again in our own weaknesses."

Morgan, Kitty, and Jerry sat in silence as they contemplated everything they had experienced together—all the internal conflicts, the worst hurricane of the century, and William's resignation. Now they understood the human potential of forgiveness and the possibility of moving to a stronger, more balanced way of leading others and in living their lives.

They were encouraged and strengthened.

Mapping Exercise #5: Your Personal Map

Now let's turn to your own experience and a time when you had difficulties with someone at work. Using the map below, list some Early Warnings that suggested that you were over-focusing on one value to the neglect of the other. Then write down the Action Steps you might take to balance the values pair of Fairness *and* Forgiveness.

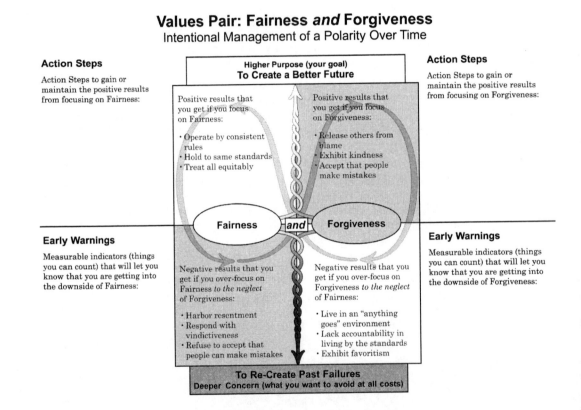

Values Pair: Fairness *and* Forgiveness
Intentional Management of a Polarity Over Time

Action Steps

Action Steps to gain or maintain the positive results from focusing on Fairness:

Action Steps

Action Steps to gain or maintain the positive results from focusing on Forgiveness:

Higher Purpose (your goal)
To Create a Better Future

Positive results that you get if you focus on Fairness:

· Operate by consistent rules
· Hold to same standards
· Treat all equitably

Positive results that you get if you focus on Forgiveness:

· Release others from blame
· Exhibit kindness
· Accept that people make mistakes

Fairness and **Forgiveness**

Early Warnings

Measurable indicators (things you can count) that will let you know that you are getting into the downside of Fairness:

Early Warnings

Measurable indicators (things you can count) that will let you know that you are getting into the downside of Forgiveness:

Negative results that you get if you over-focus on Fairness *to the neglect* of Forgiveness:

· Harbor resentment
· Respond with vindictiveness
· Refuse to accept that people can make mistakes

Negative results that you get if you over-focus on Forgiveness *to the neglect* of Fairness:

· Live in an "anything goes" environment
· Lack accountability in living by the standards
· Exhibit favoritism

To Re-Create Past Failures
Deeper Concern (what you want to avoid at all costs)

These coaching exercises show how pairs of interdependent values present themselves and suggest ways that astute leaders can balance them. In the next chapter, I will share with you a personal story that demonstrates another level at which polarities exist in each person's life.

Chapter Seven

My Power Surge

My aunt Mamie taught me early in life about the importance of being a good person. She insisted that I care for others, explaining that good southern women put other people first because that is a lady's role in society. She said that when I take care of others, I will feel good about myself and they will feel good about me. Also, if I care for others first, people will never see me as selfish (a very un-ladylike quality). Taking care of others will keep me connected— clearly the woman's responsibility.

So I lived my life caring for others. In my fifty-fourth year, I got a wake-up call. I began to ask myself what caring for others looks like for modern southern women.

Here's the picture I saw:

- *I cared for my mother during years of her declining health and hospitalization, and eventual passing.*
- *I helped out this favorite aunt with medical and transportation needs until her death.*
- *I was the only child to support my aging father.*
- *I was maintaining a wonderful home life with Bob, my husband of twenty-two years, and our cats.*
- *I was taking care of the needs of in-town clients.*
- *I was taking care of out-of-state clients, traveling great distances to do so.*
- *I was making time for friends (when I had any time left over for them).*

I'd tried to do what Aunt Mamie taught me, because I trusted her. I also wanted to do the "right" thing; I certainly wanted to avoid letting people down in their time of need, or be labeled as selfish. So my life was driven by that Motivational Value: *Care for Others*. I worked late and worked on the weekends, worked from home, and even worked from my mother's hospital room. I got sick frequently (four colds in six months) and was physically and mentally fatigued.

Joy was slipping out of my life, and I started to resent having to work all weekend while others played. I longed to be more like those people: the ones out there having fun in life.

I applied what I had learned through Polarity Management and began to see what I had done to myself. Neither Aunt Mamie nor my mother wanted me sick and joyless. They both wanted me healthy and happy!

Both taught me from what they learned about life, and neither one knew anything about managing values as interdependent pairs. But until I sat down and thought about the polarities in my own situation, I hadn't been able to see that what I was missing was the value of *Caring for Myself*.

To have a great life, I needed to Care for Others *and* Myself. If I wanted to be physically and mentally energized and engaged *as well as* experience joy in living my own life, I needed to focus on both. It was "right" to care for others *and* "right" to care for myself. The answer seems so simple in hindsight.

The *and* realization gave me a broader view from which to live my life. I understood the need to embrace both values in the pair to gain greater life balance, and knew that I would be able to manage both values simultaneously. I learned how to avoid allowing my strength to become my weakness.

Here is the Polarity Map I made for myself to find the balance:

Intentional Management of a Polarity Over Time

Action Steps

Action Steps to gain or maintain the positive results from focusing on Caring for Others:

1. Visit my father once per week
2. Spend time with Bob
3. Meet friends for lunch or dinner
4. Want to make a difference in my work
5. Ask clients and friends for feedback

Higher Purpose (your goal)
To Be a Good Human Being

Positive results that you get if you focus on Caring for Others:

· Feel good helping others
· Let others know their needs are important
· Keep connected to others

Positive results that you get if you focus on Caring for Self:

· Tend to personal needs
· Energize physically and mentally
· Enjoy doing what is important to self

Caring for Others *and* **Caring for Self**

Action Steps

Action Steps to gain or maintain the positive results from focusing on Caring for Others:

1. Teach indoor cycling and work out five times a week
2. Take vacations in concert with work engagements
3. Limit number of client work days per month
4. Attend the Polarity Management Learning Community meetings

Early Warnings

Measurable indicators (things you can count) that will let you know that you are getting into the downside of Caring for Others:

1. Unhealthy vitals/get sick frequently
2. Make errors in my job
3. Always doing something (such as work and household chores) without rest time

Negative results that you get if you over-focus on Caring for Others *to the neglect* of Caring for Self:

· Neglect personal needs
· Experience physical and mental fatigue
· Miss out on doing what is important for self

Negative results that you get if you over-focus on Caring for Self *to the neglect* of Caring for Others:

· Feel selfish
· Allow others to feel abandoned when in need
· Isolate myself

Early Warnings

Measurable indicators (things you can count) that will let you know that you are getting into the downside of Caring for Self:

1. Friends quit calling me
2. Clients quit calling me
3. Less work in pipeline
4. Can't pay my retirement contribution

To Be a Failure as a Human Being
Deeper Concern (what you want to avoid at all costs)

Putting this all down on paper clarified what I was doing to myself and helped me identify how I could balance the two.

So I ask you: What are *your* Motivational Values? Can you name a few related Interdependent Values for each one? If you haven't yet discovered values as *pairs* or polarities, this is a good opportunity for you to raise your personal and professional awareness. It will present you with a great opportunity to lead and live life *better*.

I've designed a short workbook to help you answer those questions and heighten your awareness so you can balance *your* strengths in value pairs. You'll see how easy it is!

Chapter Eight

Building and Balancing Your Leadership Strengths

Polarity Mapping Objectives

You will have a better idea of what it takes to be an effective leader if you do these six things:

1. Identify your key Motivational Values.
2. Find an Interdependent Value to supplement each Motivational Value.
3. View both values as a working pair to be managed and balanced over time.
4. Put both values on a Polarity Map so you can see the positive results and possible negative results from both values.
5. Create a plan to achieve and maintain higher performance, thereby tapping into the pair's synergy.
6. Recognize early on when you are out of balance, so that you can take corrective action.

How to Fill Out a Polarity Map

To help you as you build your own Polarity Map, I will explain and give you my example for each step. (Use the blank map on pages 86–87 to create your map, and turn to page 84 if you want to review my sample.)

1. Identify your Higher Purpose and your Deeper Concern.

(Place your answers in the top and bottom boxes
of the template on pages 86–87.)

Higher Purpose

The Higher Purpose statement appears in the box at the top of a Polarity Map. It answers the question, "Ultimately, what am I trying to achieve? What is my goal?"

For example: *To be an effective consultant.*

Deeper Concern

Deeper Concern appears in the box at the bottom of the map. It is always the opposite of the Higher Purpose statement. It's what you really want to avoid at all costs.

For example: *To be a failure as a consultant.*

2. Motivational Value Point of View

Name your Motivational Value.

(Place your answer in the left oval.)

See *Appendix A* for a list of common values and their synonyms.

Recall the earlier working definition of Motivational Values:

A Motivational Value

- Is an important quality or principle about yourself
  (for example: *Dependability*)
- Guides what you say or do
  (for example: *I keep my commitments.*)
- Represents a principle or standard that directs your actions as a leader
  (for example: *Others can rely on me as a leader to follow through, because I'm known for my word being my bond.*)

Name two or three positive results that you get if you focus on your Motivational Value.

(Place your answers in the upper left-hand quadrant of the map.)

For example: If I focus on *Dependability,* I will get these positive results:

- Feel reliable and trustworthy
- Honor deadlines and keep my promises
- Maintain a steady list of clients

For each positive result you listed, determine its negative opposite.

(Place your answers in the lower right-hand quadrant of the map.)

Consideration: These negatives might be weaknesses or fears that would make you cringe if other people think of you in this way or if this is your reputation.

For example: If I lose my focus on *Dependability,* I might get these negative results:

- Feel like a slacker
- Miss deadlines and break my promises
- Worry about losing clients

3. Interdependent Value Point of View

Identify the Interdependent Value.

(Place your answer in the right oval of the map.)

See *Appendix B* for a list of possible paired values.

For example: *Playfulness* is listed as the Interdependent Value for *Dependability.*

At this point, the value listed in *Appendix B* may not seem to fit or make sense. This isn't unusual. Continue with the mapping and see if it works for you. If not, create a word that better describes your own Interdependent Value and resonates with you.

Identify two or three potential negative results from your Motivational Value if you neglect the Interdependent Value.

(Place your answers in the lower left-hand quadrant of the map.)

Here is where you explore the missing point of view. Think of some negative results you might get if you over-focus on your Motivational Value to the neglect of the Interdependent Value. (This step may be more difficult.)

For example: If I over-focus on *Dependability* to the neglect of *Playfulness*, I might get these negative results:

- Feel pushed and stressed
- Get anxious about spending time with family and friends
- Become humorless

For each negative result you listed from over-focusing on your Motivational Value, determine its positive opposite.

(Place your answers in the upper right-hand quadrant of the map.)

These are potential positive results you can gain from a focus on the newly identified Interdependent Value.

For example, positive results that I could gain if I focus on *Playfulness:*

- Feel relaxed and refreshed
- Get excited about spending time with family and friends
- Have fun

Intentional Management of a Polarity Over Time

Action Steps

Action Steps to gain or maintain the positive results from focusing on Dependability:

Higher Purpose (your goal)
To Be an Effective Consultant

Action Steps

Action Steps to gain or maintain the positive results from focusing on Playfulness:

Positive results that you get if you focus on Dependability:

- Feel reliable and trustworthy
- Honor deadlines, keep promises
- Maintain a steady list of clients

Positive results that you get if you focus on Playfulness:

- Feel relaxed and refreshed
- Get excited about spending time with family and friends
- Have fun

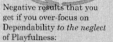

Dependability and **Playfulness**

Early Warnings

Measurable indicators (things you can count) that will let you know that you are getting into the downside of Dependability:

Early Warnings

Measurable indicators (things you can count) that will let you know that you are getting into the downside of Playfulness:

Negative results that you get if you over-focus on Dependability *to the neglect* of Playfulness:

- Feel pushed and stressed
- Get anxious about spending time with family and friends
- Become humorless

Negative results that you get if you over-focus on Playfulness *to the neglect* of Dependability:

- Feel like a slacker
- Miss deadlines and break my promises
- Worry about losing clients

To Be a Failure as a Consultant
Deeper Concern (what you want to avoid at all costs)

4. Intentional Management of a Polarity Over Time

The expanded Polarity Map on this page shows you how to be intentional in managing and balancing the results you get from both values over time. To raise and sustain higher levels of performance, you must gain the positive results from both values simultaneously, *and* you must recognize those times when you need to shift your focus in order to minimize or avoid experiencing negative results.

Action Steps

To maximize performance from a polarity, establish a way to maintain a balance between the two values. Continue to focus on those values, and do what has enabled you to gain the positive results of your Motivational Value in the past. **It is important to list these things as Action Steps on your map so you can continue to achieve those positive results.** It's simply being clear about what you already do. Acknowledging what you do now—which will continue to serve you well in the future—keeps you from over-focusing on the newly identified Interdependent Value.

(Place these action steps in the upper-left corner of the map.)

For example, the Action Steps I will continue to take in order to maintain the positive results of *Dependability:*

1. Make and keep specific agreements
2. Schedule in-office work hours
3. Let clients know what they can expect from me

Next, create a new set of Action Steps to help you intentionally get the positives of your newly discovered Interdependent Value.

(Place in upper-right corner.)

For example, Action Steps I will begin to take to gain the positive results of *Playfulness:*

1. Schedule commitments that can be completed during set office hours
2. Attend one social event per week

3. Read one mystery novel per month
4. Teach a yoga class for friends

Early Warnings

Finally, it's important to have a way to tell when your focus may be getting out of balance. Early Warnings are measurable indicators that alert you to being over-focused on one value to the neglect of the other, so that you can change focus to re-gain balance. The earlier the warning, the faster you can prevent any negative results.

Identify several Early Warnings to alert you that you are focusing too much on your Motivational Value and neglecting the Interdependent Value.

(Place these in the lower left-hand corner on your map.)

For example, indicators to help me recognize that I am over-focusing on *Dependability:*

1. Interested only in discussing my work
2. Staying up late into the night or working all weekend to meet commitments
3. Unwilling to attend social functions
4. Clients feel pushed by me

Identify several Early Warnings to alert you that you are overfocusing on the Interdependent Value and neglecting your Motivational Value.

(Place these in the lower right-hand corner of your map.)

For example, indicators to help me recognize I am over-focusing on *Playfulness:*

1. More broken commitments to clients
2. Increase in the number of client complaints
3. Decrease in number of word-of-mouth referrals

Now that you understand how I worked out my Early Warnings and Action Steps to keep the polarities in balance, look at the completed Polarity Map on the next page to see how everything fits together.

Intentional Management of a Polarity Over Time

Action Steps

Action Steps to gain or maintain the positive results from focusing on Dependability:

1. Make and keep specific agreements
2. Schedule in-office work hours
3. Let clients know what they can expect from me

Action Steps

Action Steps to gain or maintain the positive results from focusing on Playfulness:

1. Schedule commitments that can be completed during set office hours
2. Attend one social event per week
3. Read one mystery novel per month
4. Teach a yoga class for friends

Higher Purpose (your goal)
To Be an Effective Consultant

Positive results that you get if you focus on Dependability:

- Feel reliable and trustworthy
- Honor deadlines, keep promises
- Maintain a steady list of clients

Positive results that you get if you focus on Playfulness:

- Feel relaxed and refreshed
- Get excited about spending time with family and friends
- Have fun

Dependability and **Playfulness**

Negative results that you get if you over-focus on Dependability *to the neglect* of Playfulness:

- Feel pushed and stressed
- Get anxious about spending time with family and friends
- Become humorless

Negative results that you get if you over-focus on Playfulness *to the neglect* of Dependability:

- Feel like a slacker
- Miss deadlines and break my promises
- Worry about losing clients

To Be a Failure as a Consultant
Deeper Concern (what you want to avoid at all costs)

Early Warnings

Measurable indicators (things you can count) that will let you know that you are getting into the downside of Dependability:

1. Interested only in discussing my work
2. Staying up late into the night, or working all weekend to meet commitments
3. Unwilling to attend social functions
4. Clients feel pushed by me

Early Warnings

Measurable indicators (things you can count) that will let you know that you are getting into the downside of Playfulness:

1. More broken commitments to clients
2. Increase in the number of client complaints
3. Decrease in number of word-of-mouth referrals

Important Reminder

The Infinity Loop stands for the ongoing need to balance. You must remember that there must be an ongoing dynamic energy between the two values if you are to get the best out of both of them and create the synergy needed to move you to a higher level of performance. It is important to be very clear about the positive results to be gained from both values, as well as the potential negative results from being out-of-balance, but I cannot over-stress the central role of the infinity loop.

> The infinity loop is essential, because it demonstrates the ongoing need to balance.

The infinity loop provides us with a constant reminder that the most basic elements of a polarity are the two poles and the infinite energy system in which they are dynamically held.

Polarity Mapping Templates

Intentional Management of a Polarity Over Time

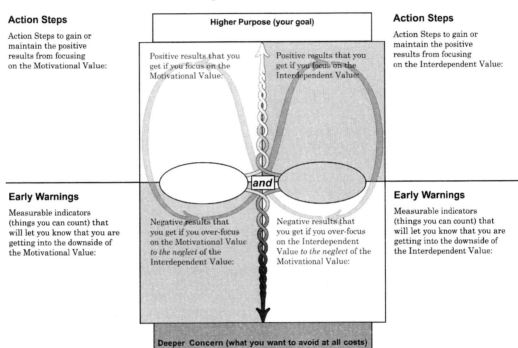

Action Steps

Action Steps to gain or
maintain the positive
results from focusing
on the Motivational Value:

Action Steps

Action Steps to gain or
maintain the positive
results from focusing
on the Interdependent Value:

Higher Purpose (your goal)

Positive results that you
get if you focus on the
Motivational Value:

Positive results that you
get if you focus on the
Interdependent Value:

and

Early Warnings

Measurable indicators
(things you can count) that
will let you know that you are
getting into the downside of
the Motivational Value:

Early Warnings

Measurable indicators
(things you can count) that
will let you know that you are
getting into the downside of
the Interdependent Value:

Negative results that
you get if you over-focus
on the Motivational Value
to the neglect of the
Interdependent Value:

Negative results that
you get if you over-focus
on the Interdependent
Value *to the neglect* of the
Motivational Value:

Deeper Concern (what you want to avoid at all costs)

Intentional Management of a Polarity Over Time

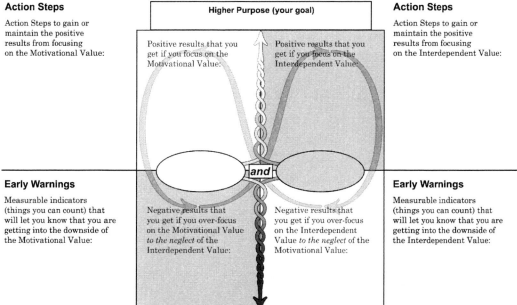

Action Steps

Action Steps to gain or
maintain the positive
results from focusing
on the Motivational Value:

Higher Purpose (your goal)

Positive results that you
get if you focus on the
Motivational Value:

Positive results that you
get if you focus on the
Interdependent Value:

Action Steps

Action Steps to gain or
maintain the positive
results from focusing
on the Interdependent Value:

and

Early Warnings

Measurable indicators
(things you can count) that
will let you know that you are
getting into the downside of
the Motivational Value:

Negative results that
you get if you over-focus
on the Motivational Value
to the neglect of the
Interdependent Value:

Negative results that
you get if you over-focus
on the Interdependent
Value *to the neglect* of the
Motivational Value:

Early Warnings

Measurable indicators
(things you can count) that
will let you know that you are
getting into the downside of
the Interdependent Value:

Deeper Concern (what you want to avoid at all costs)

Conclusion

For more than 4,000 years, philosophers and religious teachers have been writing about the fundamental realities of life. The concept of yin and yang, which surfaced in Chinese philosophy approximately 2,500 years ago, refers to two opposing and complementary elements of any one complex phenomenon. Together, those two elements create something larger or better than the two parts individually. Yin-yang exists in a dynamic equilibrium: As one element declines, the other increases to an equal degree. This philosophy of balance is still practiced in traditional Chinese medicine.

Polarity Management takes this same idea and brings it into our world today. It creates a simpler way for us to grasp and talk about those ongoing, complex issues we face in our human experience on earth.

It's only been in the last few decades that business leaders have recognized the potential in being able to understand and manage polarities. A leader's ability to see and hold two very different points of view simultaneously not only changes how the leader sees and thinks, but it also provides more and richer options when dealing with tough people and the tough realities faced in organizational life.

The story in *Power Surge* shows us what leaders experience when they are unable to see more than one point of view. It can be disastrous for the leader, the employees, and a community.

I should know about *disastrous*. For many years, I worked as a manager who had only one set of beliefs about how things should be done—mine. And I followed those beliefs closely. After all, I thought I was doing things "right."

Here was my pattern: Things would be going smoothly with my employees for a while, and lots of work would get accomplished. Then, without seeing it coming, the wheels would come off, and I would find myself vilified by those same employees. Now I recognize the pattern I created: I was over-focusing on Task and neglecting the importance of Relationships with people who get the work done.

What changed for me, when I learned about Polarity Management, was this: I realized that if I wanted to be a better leader, I needed to supplement my natural tendency to focus on Task with something very different, yet complementary: Relationships.

I now challenge *you* to examine *your* approach and tap into the power of *and* in your leadership life and beyond.

Note: To continue your growth and support your learning through a community of leaders, go to www.mypowersurge.com. Password is **BALANCE** to join the interactive forum.

Appendix A

Motivational Values

Motivational Values

Motivational values are important qualities or principles that guide what we say and do and direct our actions.

Scan the list of Motivational Values and their clarifying descriptors and synonyms.

Then select a Motivational Value OR its synonym that you closely identify with, and pay close attention to finding a word that resonates with you.

Motivational Value	Value Clarification Descriptors/Synonyms
1. accountability	responsibility, answerability, liability
2. achievement	accomplishment, attainment, success, completion, realization
3. aesthetics	consideration of appearance and beauty, style
4. altruism	unselfishness, selflessness, philanthropy, charity
5. autonomy	independence, self-sufficiency, self-government, self-rule
6. balance	equilibrium, steadiness, stability
7. being the best	greatness, finest, unsurpassed, top, paramount, preeminent
8. candor	integrity, truth, truthfulness, honor, veracity, uprightness
9. caution	care, concern, watchfulness, prudence, vigilance, safety
10. change	alter, modify, vary, transform, revolutionize, adjust
11. clarity	simplicity, lucidity, transparence
12. collaboration	partnership, group effort, association, alliance, cooperation
13. commitment	promise, pledge, vow, obligation, assurance, binder
14. common sense	decisions guided by experience and intuition
15. communication	exchange of ideas, interaction, interchange, discourse, discussion
16. community service	provide service outside your organization
17. compassion	sympathy, empathy, concern, kindness, consideration, care
18. competence	capability, skill, fitness, proficiency, know-how, expertise
19. competition	challenge, stay/get ahead of others, meet customer demands
20. confidence	self-assurance, poise, knowing who you are

(continued)

Motivational Value	Value Clarification Descriptors/Synonyms
21. consensus	agreement, accord, harmony, compromise, consent
22. consistency	predictability of actions or words
23. control	manage, organize, be in charge of, have power over, be in command of
24. courage	bravery, guts, nerve, valor, daring, audacity
25. creativity	originality, inventiveness, ingenuity, breaking boundaries
26. customer service	taking care of the customer is of prime importance
27. delegation	allocation, designation, handing over, giving out, passing on
28. dependability	reliability, constancy, steadiness
29. direction	define expectations and elements of mission, goals, tasks
30. discipline	regulation, order, control, restraint, obedience, authority
31. diversity	variety, assortment, multiplicity, mixture—work and life styles
32. efficiency	doing things right, eliminating waste and improving materials and processes
33. effectiveness	doing right things, challenging current paths and changing when needed
34. emergence	provide freedom for creativity of new ideas, self-organization
35. empathy	understanding, sympathy, compassion, "walking in another's shoes"
36. empowerment	people/teams have information, resources, and opportunity to make a difference
37. enthusiasm	eagerness, interest, keenness, fervor, passion, gusto, zeal, zest
38. ecological care	safeguarding the planet; honoring and preserving all life and habitat
39. equality	fairness, equal opportunity, impartiality, individual rights
40. fairness	justice, equity, impartiality, individual rights
41. flexibility	adaptable, accommodating, variable, open to change
42. forgiveness	pardon, clemency, pity, mercy, absolution, amnesty, exoneration
43. personal fulfillment	satisfaction, contentment, happiness, and joy in own work and play
44. future-focused	forward-thinking, legacy-minded

(continued)

Power Surge

Motivational Value	Value Clarification Descriptors/Synonyms
45. growth	enlargement, increase, expansion, development
46. harmony	agreement, accord, concord, synchronization, unity, peace
47. humor/fun	work is enjoyable, entertaining, pleasurable
48. humility	modesty, unassuming nature, share praise, take blame when due
49. image	importance of impression, status, picture held by others
50. inclusion	including, admitting, integration, combination
51. independence	individuality, uniqueness, eccentricity, distinctiveness
52. individual effort	work alone, excel in meeting needs of others
53. influence	power to affect people, things, and events, especially without visible effort
54. initiator	self-starter, determination to try, doing without directives
55. innovation	novelty, modernism, modernization, improvement, advance, originality
56. integration	addition, mixing, incorporation, combination, assimilation
57. integrity	honesty, truth, truthfulness, honor, veracity, reliability, uprightness, ethics
58. interdependence	recognize, consider our reliance and effect on human and other systems
59. justice	fairness, impartiality, righteousness, evenhandedness, fair dealing
60. leading edge	first with new products and services, think and do the new before others
61. learner	gaining wisdom, knowledge, skills, ability to discern
62. listener	understanding, comprehending, making meaning
63. logic	reason, judgment, to rely on cause and effect analysis, problem solving
64. loyalty	faithfulness, devotion, allegiance, trustworthiness, constancy, reliability
65. long-term	make decisions respecting future and business continuance
66. meaning	higher purpose, work has meaning beyond material gratification
67. mentor	individually guiding others to greater understanding and ability

(continued)

Motivational Value	Value Clarification Descriptors/Synonyms
68. openness	honesty, directness, frankness, sincerity, candidness
69. optimism	hopefulness, cheerfulness, ability to see beyond tragedy
70. order	orderliness, neatness, laws and regulations, defined method and process
71. participation	contribution, input, sharing, partaking, membership, involvement
72. perfection	accomplishment without flaws, performing to limits of ability
73. perseverance	determination, resolve, insistence, keep on keeping on
74. planning	thorough mindfulness before doing—define purpose, path, and outcome
75. power	authority, control, influence, supremacy, rule, command, dominance
76. profit	revenue beyond cost, betterment, reward for effort
77. reality	realism, actuality, authenticity, truth, certainty, veracity
78. recognition	credit, gratitude, acknowledgement, thanks, appreciation, respect
79. reflection	taking time to contemplate situations, actions, meaning, alternatives
80. relationship	association, connection with others, affiliation, rapport, bonding
81. respect	show consideration for, appreciate, regard, have a high regard for
82. results	high performance, outcome of effort, realities of new state
83. risk-taking	freedom to experiment, free to fail, adventuresome
84. short-term	focus on immediate and mid-term purpose, planning, and results
85. stability	constancy, steadiness, firmness, solidity, permanence
86. spirituality	connection to the unknown, mystery, the unanswerable questions
87. spontaneity	freedom to react to instinct and intuition to new opportunity
88. support	back up, encourage, help, assist, mentor
89. sustainability	maintain, continue, carry on, keep going, uphold, prolong
90. swiftness	speed, haste, hustle, get things done

(continued)

Motivational Value	Value Clarification Descriptors/Synonyms
91. tact	diplomacy, discretion, gracious, thoughtful, sensitive
92. task	element of work, assignment, part of larger project
93. teaching	providing skills, information, knowledge to self and others
94. teamwork	cooperation, collaboration, joint effort, solidarity
95. tradition	honoring the history, past effort, successes, custom, ritual, practices
96. trust	believe in, rely on, depend on, confide in, have confidence in
97. walk the talk	one's actions support what is said and written
98. wisdom	deep understanding, insight, perception, discernment, caring

Appendix B

Interdependent Values

Interdependent Values

Here's how to use this list when making a Polarity Map:

First, in the left-hand column, locate the Motivational Value you selected from Appendix A. It can be a synonym of the word representing your Motivational Value below.

In the right-hand column are possible Interdependent Values for your Motivational Value. Remember: An Interdependent Value supplements and balances your Motivational Value to create higher performance.

Next, consider using the suggested Interdependent Value to determine if it fits the overall potential positive results you list for Step 3, page 79 of your Polarity Map.

For additional support: go to www.mypowersurge.com. Password is **BALANCE** to join the interactive forum.

Motivational Value	*and*	Interdependent Value
1. accountability		freedom
2. achievement		celebration
3. aesthetics		functionality
4. altruism		care for self
5. autonomy		reliant on others
6. balance		choosing
7. being the best		doing the best
8. candor		diplomacy
9. caution		boldness
10. change		stability
11. clarity		flexibility
12. collaboration		competition
13. commitment		options
14. common sense		facts
15. communication		hold information
16. community service		service to self
17. compassion		detachment
18. competence		being, unconditional respect
19. competition		cooperation
20. confidence		humility
21. consensus		independent thinking
22. consistency		adaptability
23. control		empowerment
24. courage		caution

(continued)

25.	creativity	standardization
26.	customer service	service to organization
27.	delegation	guidance
28.	dependability	playfulness
29.	direction	participation
30.	discipline	freedom
31.	diversity	homogeneity
32.	efficiency	quality
33.	effectiveness	cost
34.	emergence	maintenance of what is
35.	empathy	detachment
36.	empowerment	control
37.	enthusiasm	reservation
38.	ecological care	self-interest
39.	equality	differentiation
40.	fairness	special treatment
41.	flexibility	structure
42.	forgiveness	fairness
43.	personal fulfillment	professional fulfillment
44.	future-focused	present-day focused
45.	growth	preservation
46.	harmony	divergence
47.	humor/fun	seriousness
48.	humility	confidence
49.	image	substance
50.	inclusion	exclusion
51.	independence	connectedness
52.	individual effort	group effort
53.	influence	freedom to explore
54.	initiator	follower
55.	innovation	tradition
56.	integration	differentiation
57.	integrity	diplomacy
58.	interdependence	self-reliance
59.	justice	mercy
60.	leading edge	improve what is
61.	learner	teacher
62.	listener	speaker
63.	logic	creativity
64.	loyalty	true to self
65.	long-term	short-term
66.	meaning	method
67.	mentor	learner
68.	openness	discretion
69.	optimism	realism
70.	order	emergence

(continued)

Motivational Value	*and*	Interdependent Value
71. participation		observation
72. perfection		unconditional love
73. perseverance		time for reflection
74. planning		implementation
75. power		accommodation
76. profit		intrinsic reward
77. reality		ideal
78. recognition		critical analysis
79. reflection		action
80. relationship		task
81. respect		challenge
82. results		process
83. risk-taking		protecting
84. short-term		long-term
85. spirituality		temporality
86. spontaneity		planning
87. stability		change
88. support		freedom to fail
89. sustainability		innovation
90. swiftness		mindfulness
91. tact		candor
92. task		relationship
93. teacher		learner
94. teamwork		individual work
95. tradition		change
96. trust		well grounded
97. walk the talk		talk the walk
98. wisdom		child-like inquiry

About the Author

Margaret Seidler is an organization development consultant and certified master trainer based in Charleston, South Carolina. Her professional experience ranges from organizational development work in corporations, community organizations, and a public utility to serving as staff in both houses of the South Carolina Legislature and holding planning and grants positions in county government. As a Master Trainer, she has led management teams and trained trainers in such areas as team building, coaching, and continuous process improvement.

Her interest in helping other professionals become more-effective leaders began in the 1990s, when she recognized the need to improve her own leadership skills. She was working at the time for a local electric and gas utility, and it was this experience that became the basis for the case scenario described in this book. Her consulting practice focuses on creating higher organization performance by helping clients manage the complexities of organizational leadership through the use of Polarity Management and other techniques and helping them hone their leadership skills.

Margaret holds a Master's degree in Public Administration and a Bachelor of Arts in Psychology from the University of South Carolina. Since returning to her hometown in 2001, she has presented at national and regional conferences and written for several professional publications, and has been working with individual and corporate clients nationwide. Toastmasters International profiled her in its March 2004 magazine.

Margaret lives in Charleston with her husband Bob, and is active in several business and non-profit organizations close to her heart. *Power Surge* is her first book.

She can be contacted at www.mypowersurge.com.